MW00699825

A JOURNEY THROUGH THE JUNGLE

Emily Wallis is an illustrator who uses traditional hand-drawn techniques. She completed her MA in Sequential Design and Illustration at the University of Brighton.

Also illustrated by Emily Wallis

A Sea Voyage

Anti-Stress Dot-to-Dot

The Silver Pony Ranch series
by D. L. Green

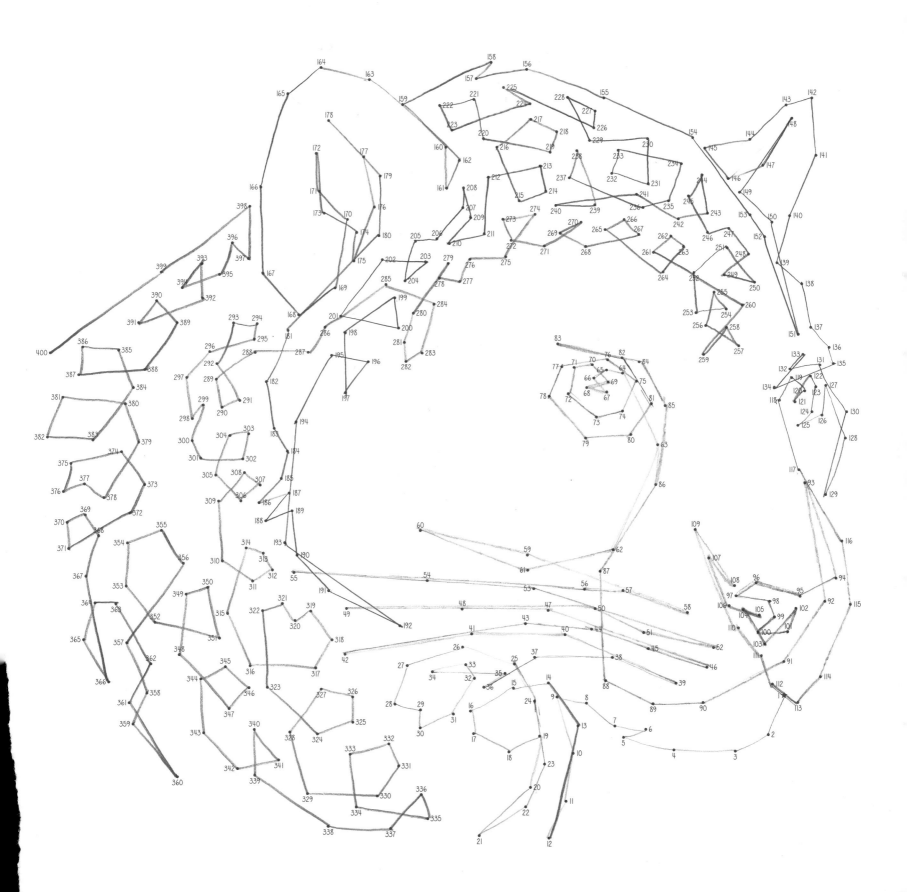

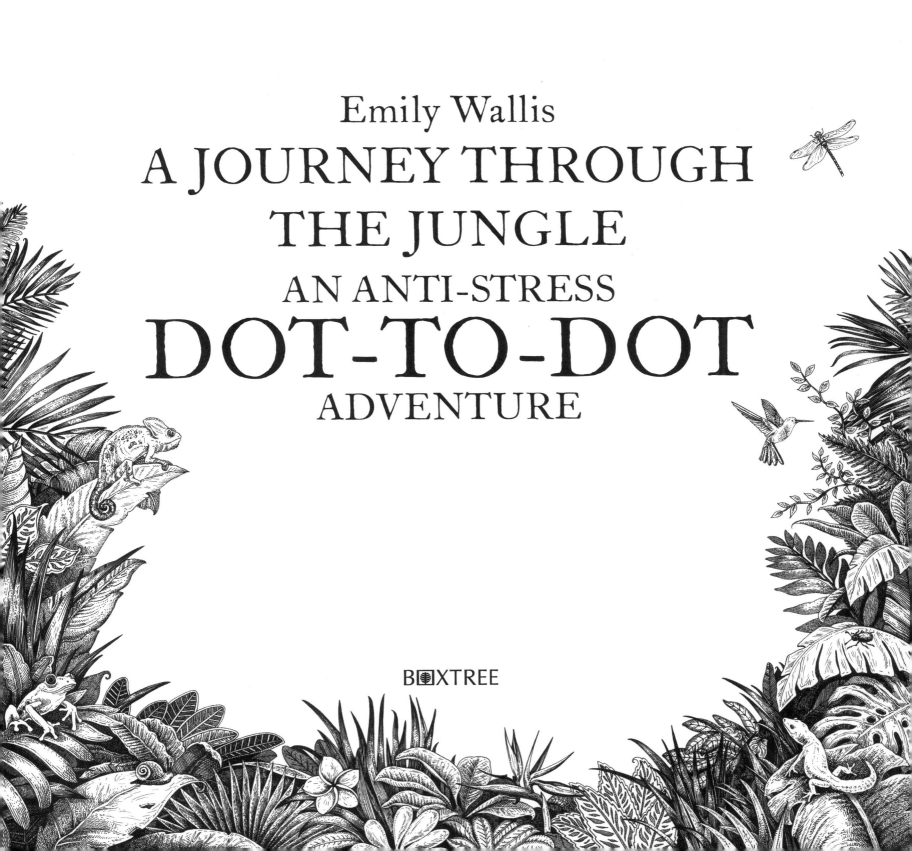

Emily Wallis

A JOURNEY THROUGH THE JUNGLE

AN ANTI-STRESS
DOT-TO-DOT
ADVENTURE

BOXTREE

First published 2016 by Boxtree
an imprint of Pan Macmillan
20 New Wharf Road, London N1 9RR
Associated companies throughout the world
www.panmacmillan.com

ISBN 978-0-7522-6621-3

Copyright © Emily Wallis 2016

The right of Emily Wallis to be identified as the
author of this work has been asserted by her in accordance
with the Copyright, Designs and Patents Act 1988.

All rights reserved. No part of this publication may be reproduced,
stored in a retrieval system, or transmitted, in any form, or by any means
(electronic, mechanical, photocopying, recording or otherwise)
without the prior written permission of the publisher.

Pan Macmillan does not have any control over, or any responsibility for,
any author or third-party websites referred to in or on this book.

1 3 5 7 9 8 6 4 2

A CIP catalogue record for this book is available from the British Library.

Printed and bound by CPI Group (UK) Ltd, Croydon, CR0 4YY

This book is sold subject to the condition that it shall not, by way of
trade or otherwise, be lent, hired out, or otherwise circulated without
the publisher's prior consent in any form of binding or cover other than
that in which it is published and without a similar condition including
this condition being imposed on the subsequent purchaser.

Visit **www.panmacmillan.com** to read more about all our books
and to buy them. You will also find features, author interviews and
news of any author events, and you can sign up for e-newsletters
so that you're always first to hear about our new releases.

Clamber into the jeep for your dot-to-dot adventure! We are about to trek through rich vegetation, surrounded by the chirp of insects and sound of bird calls.

Guided creativity is one of the best ways to slip away from the anxieties of the day and this beautiful dot-to-dot book from Emily Wallis will help you escape into the towering trees of a world inhabited by unusual flora and fauna, from the sluggish sloth to a slowly drifting dragonfly.

Each picture will take around fifteen minutes to complete. Don't worry too much about hitting the dots precisely, and don't panic if you make a mistake – one missed line won't ruin the overall picture. Be mindful of the pen in your hand and the emerging image in front of you as the rhythm of connecting the numbers begins to soothe you.

When you have your eye in, you might want to think of ways to personalize the drawings, perhaps by roughly sketching the lines with pencil, or working more precisely with an inky pen. Different methods will offer a slightly different result every time. Once you finish your image, it's time to add colour! And why not add a backdrop with some drawings of your own to complete the scene?

Every image offers a new opportunity to de-stress and be creative.

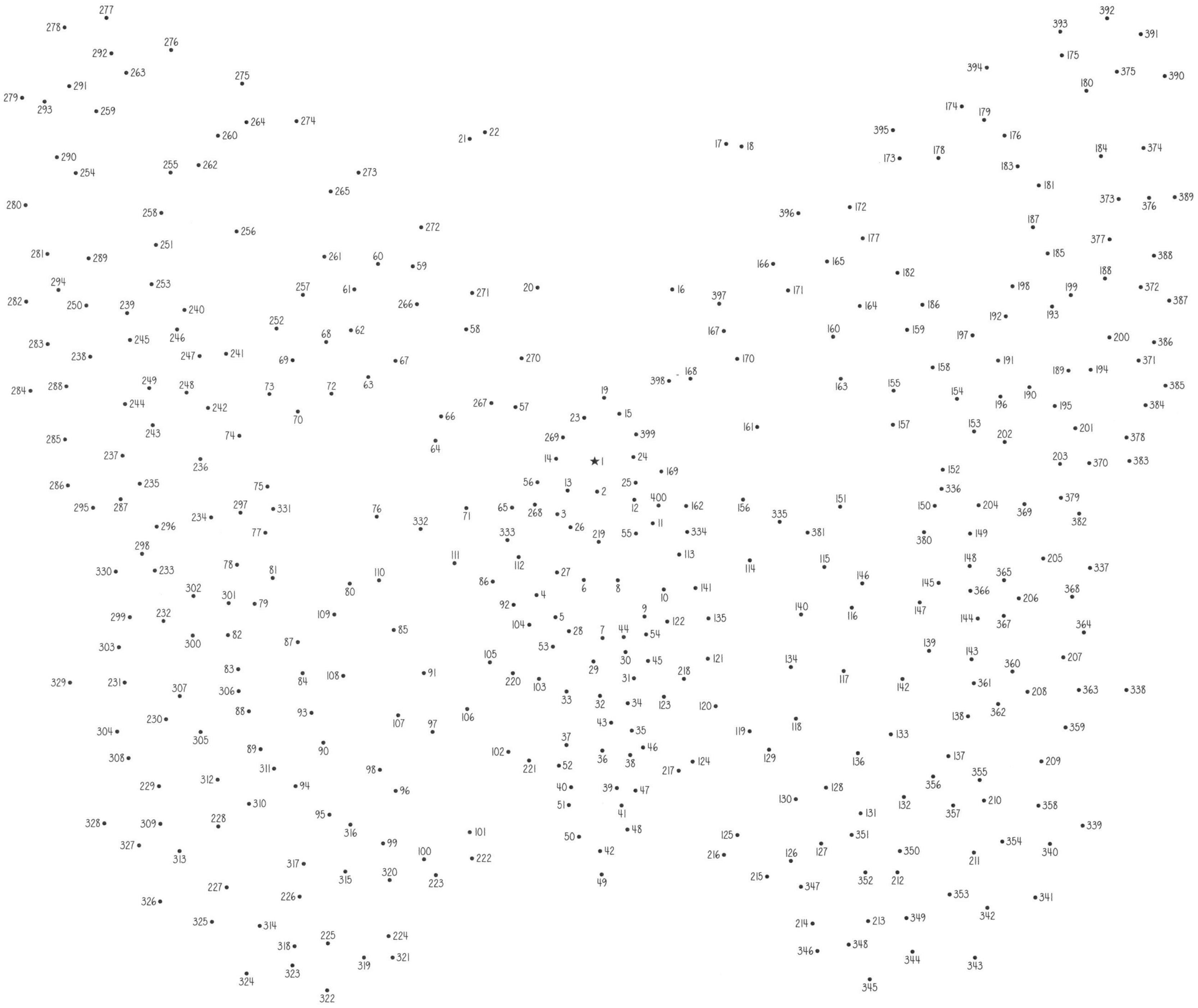

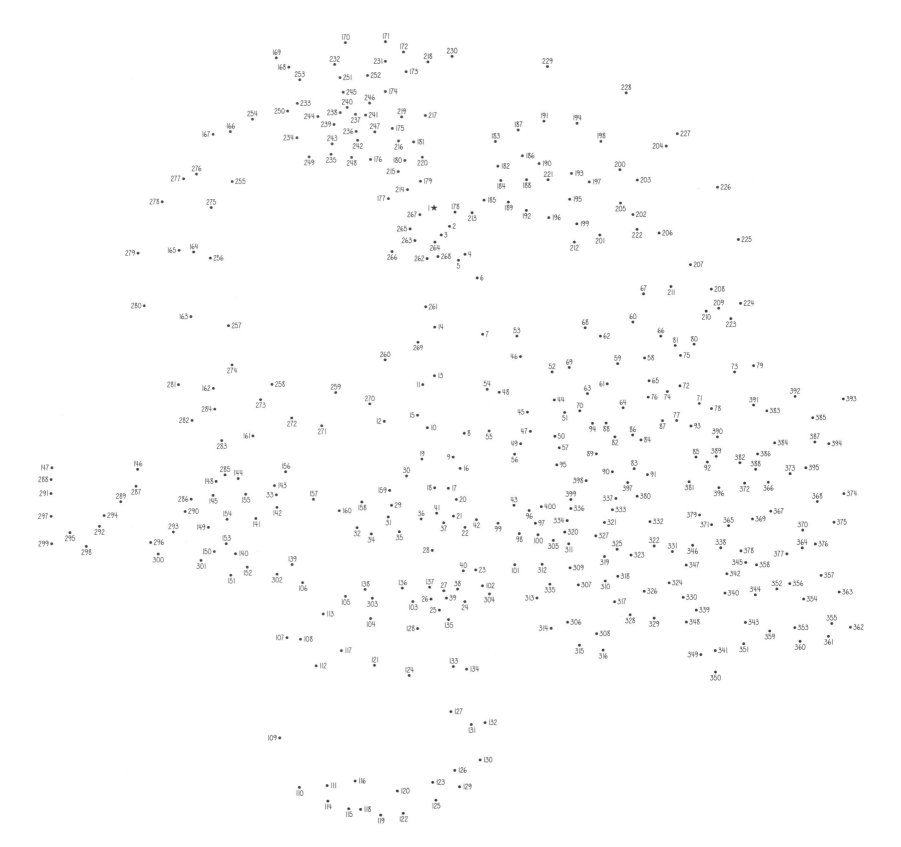

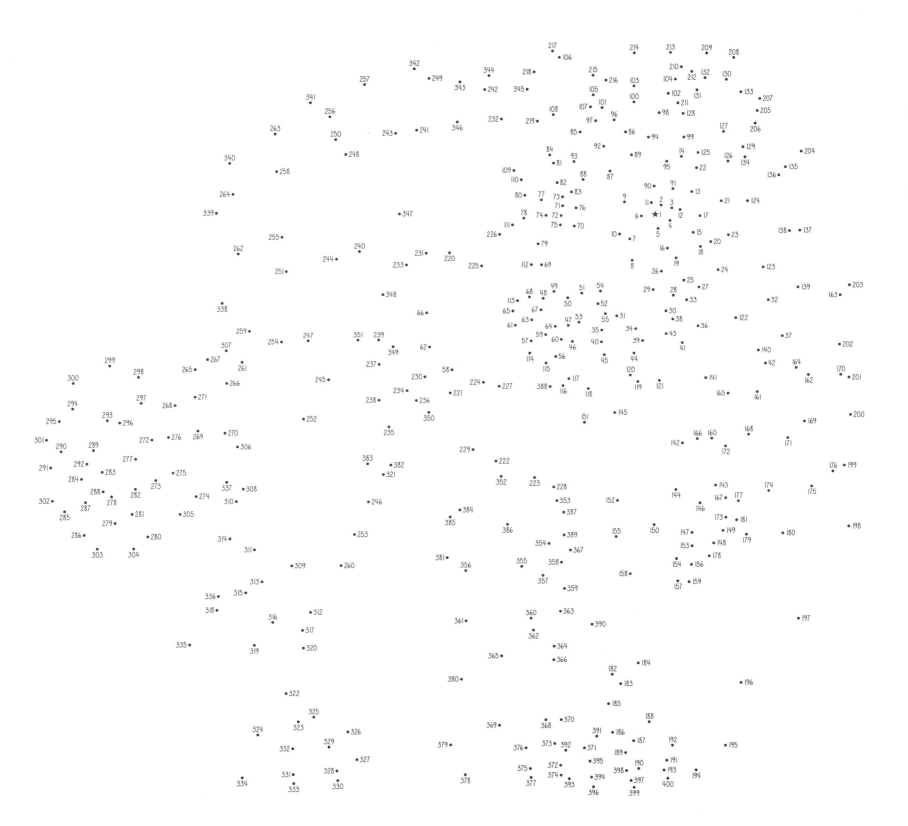

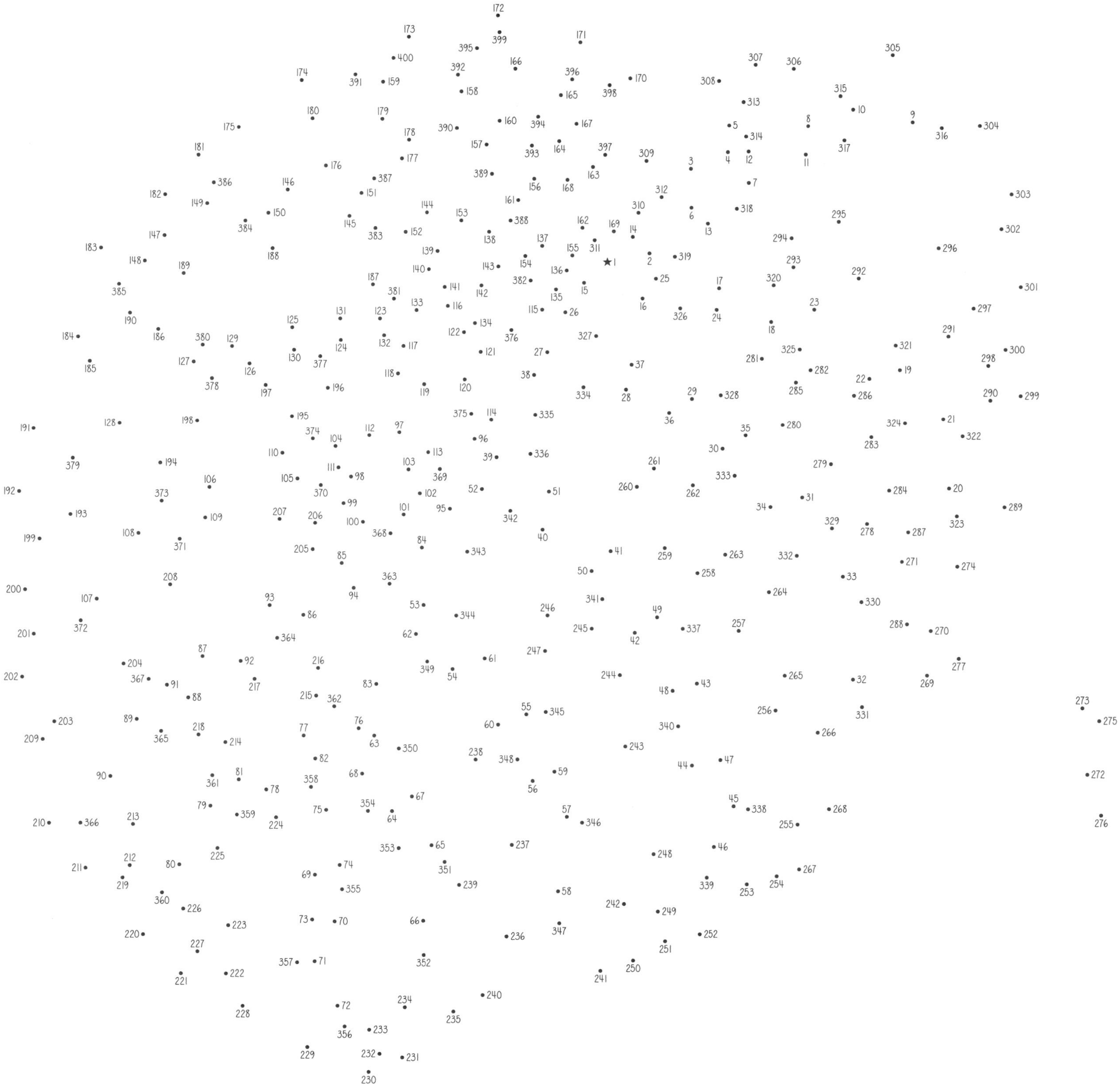

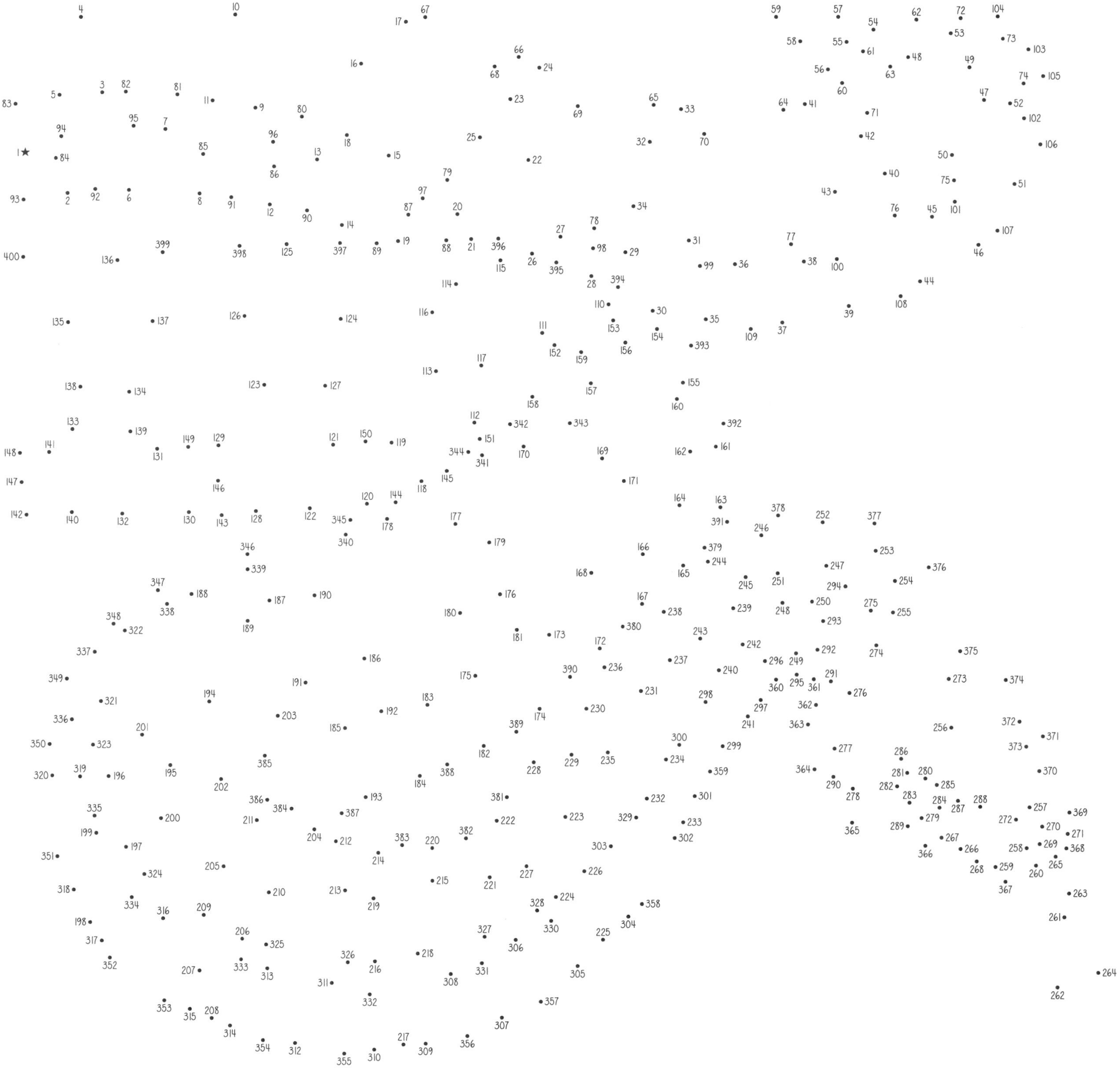

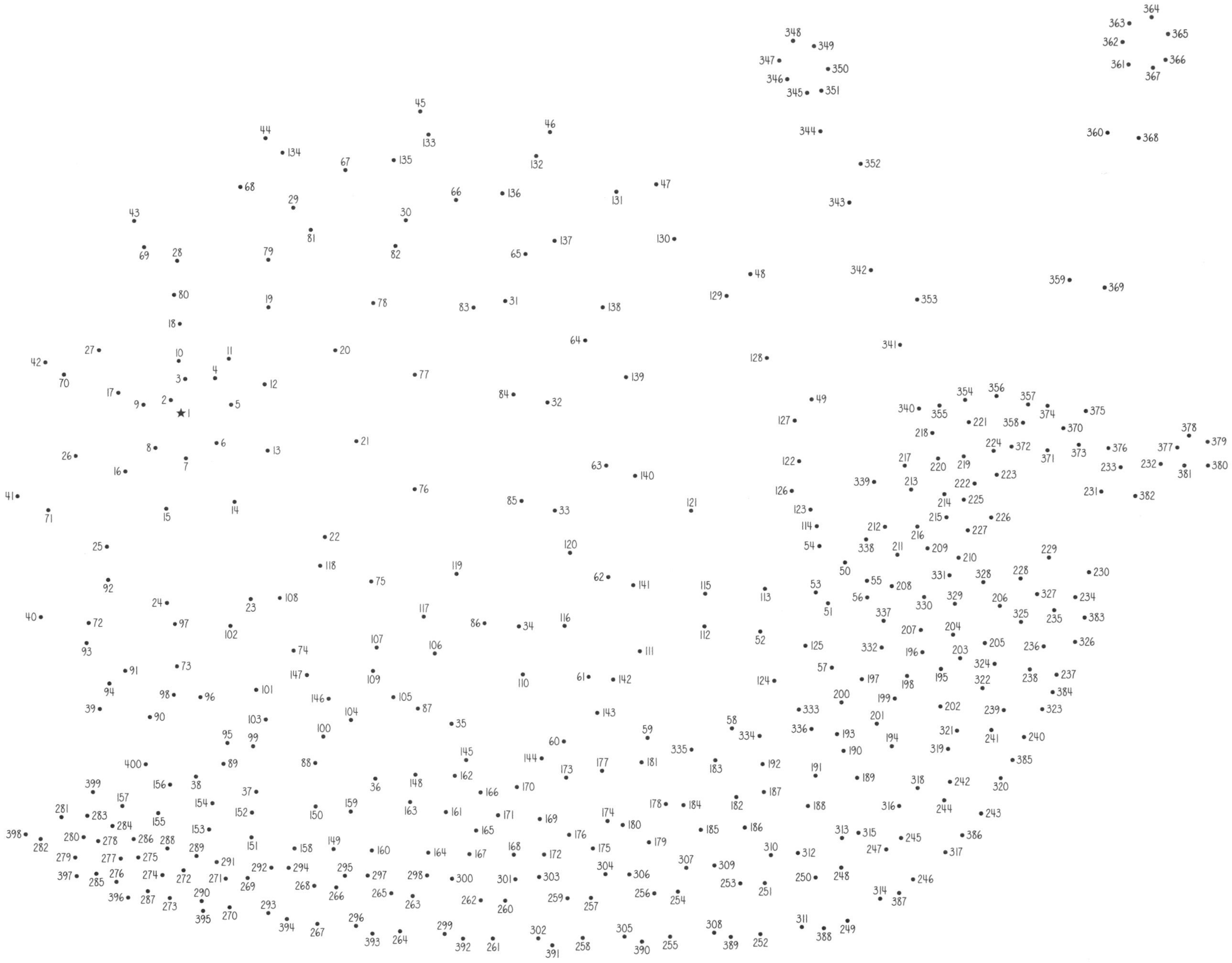

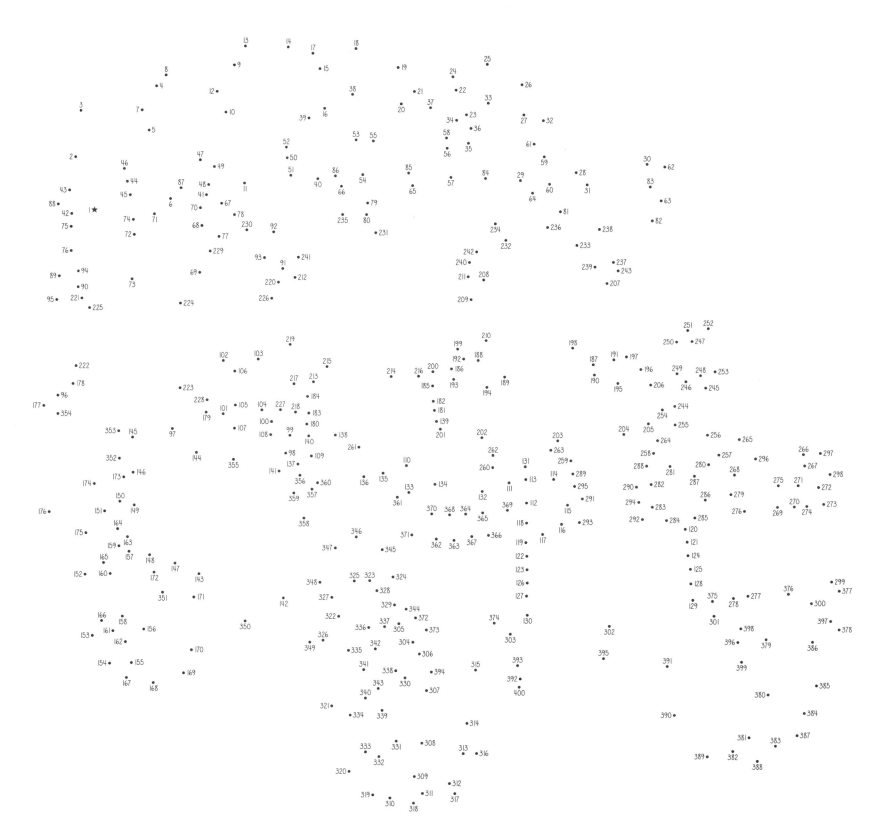

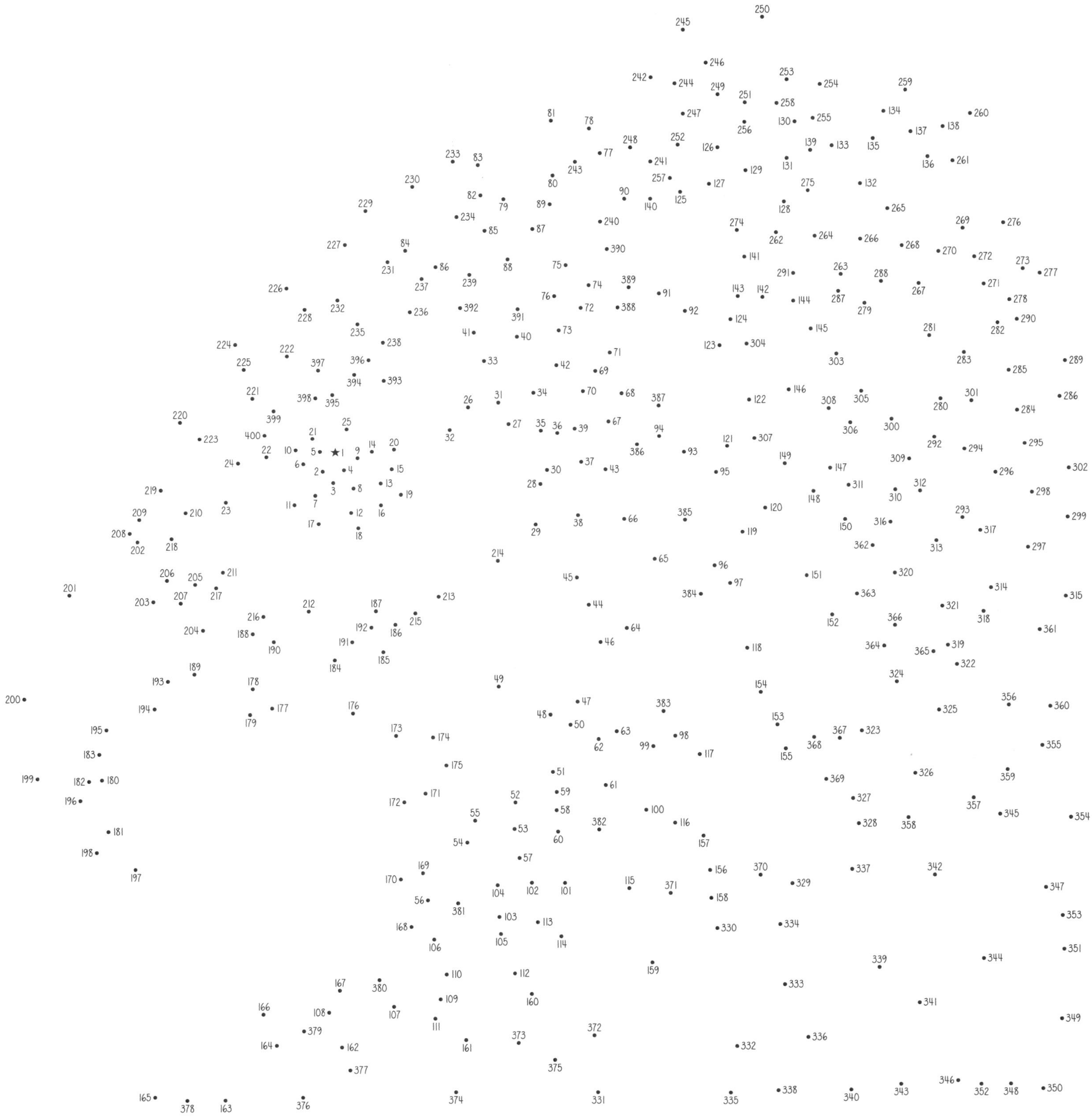

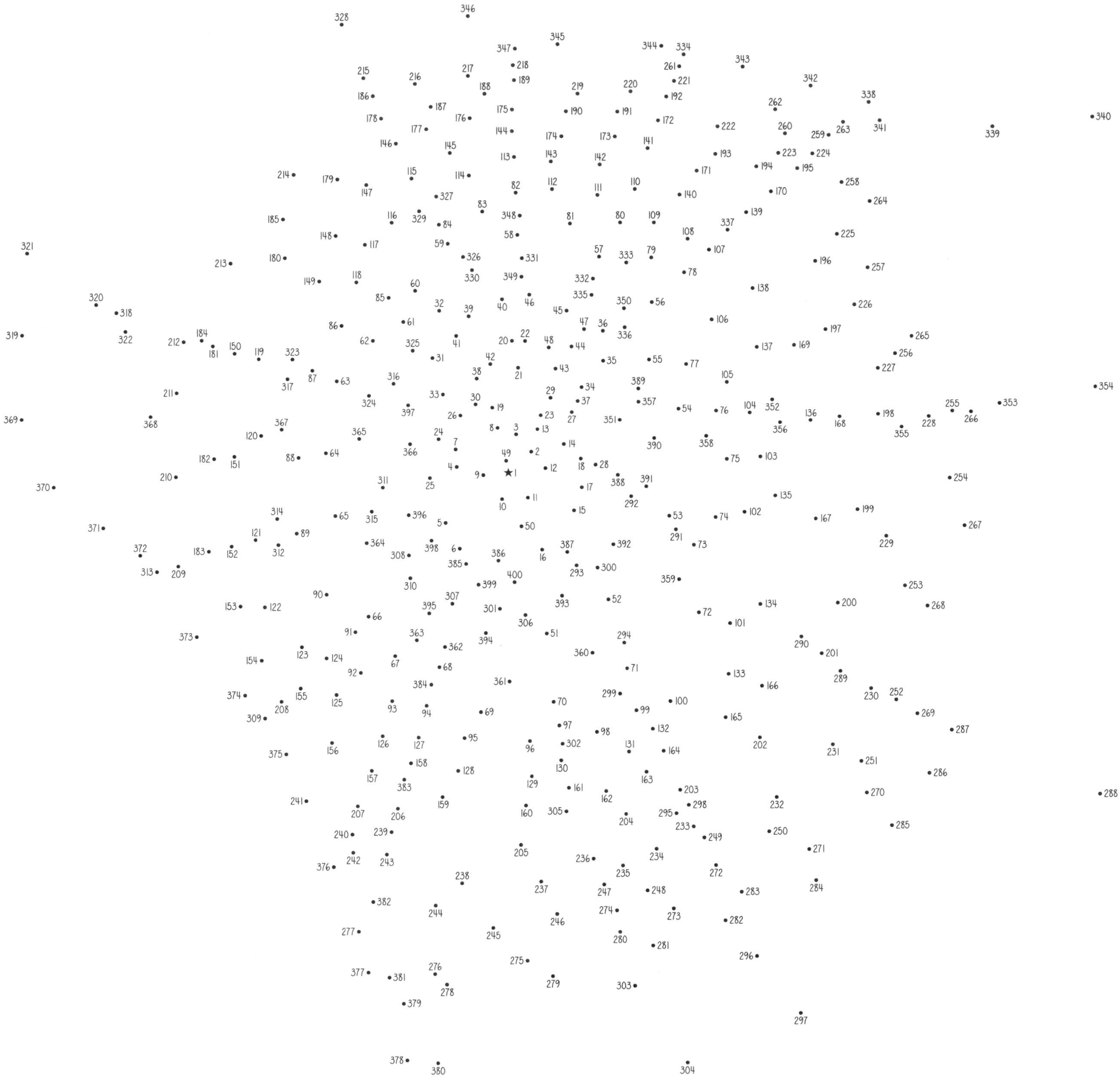

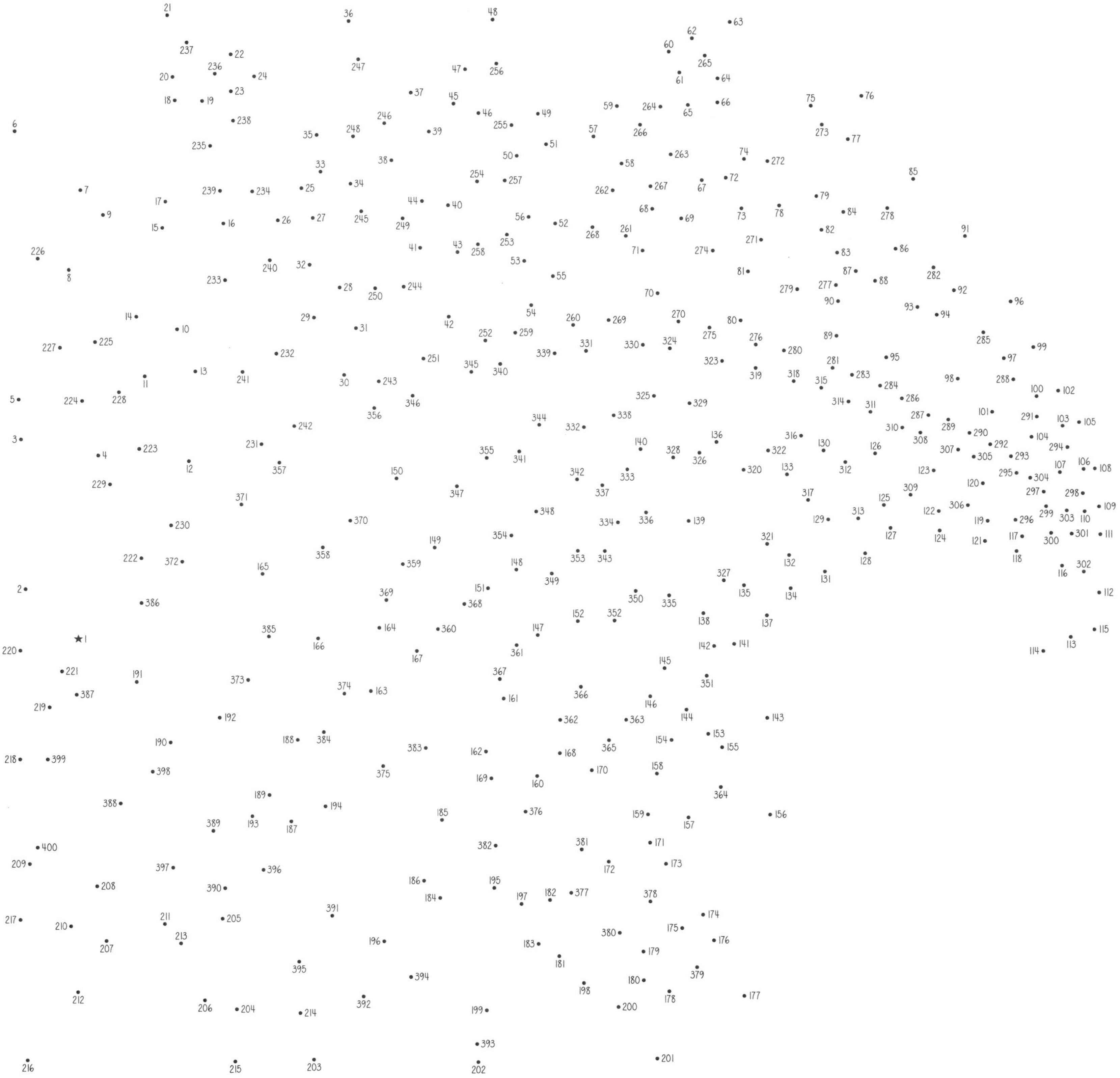

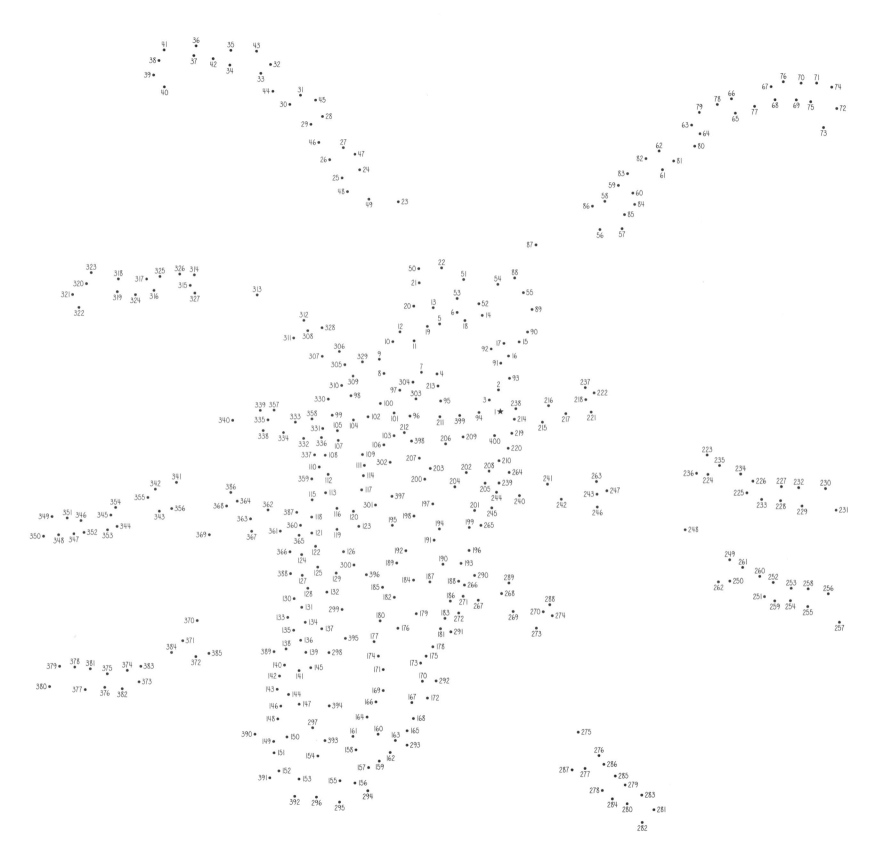

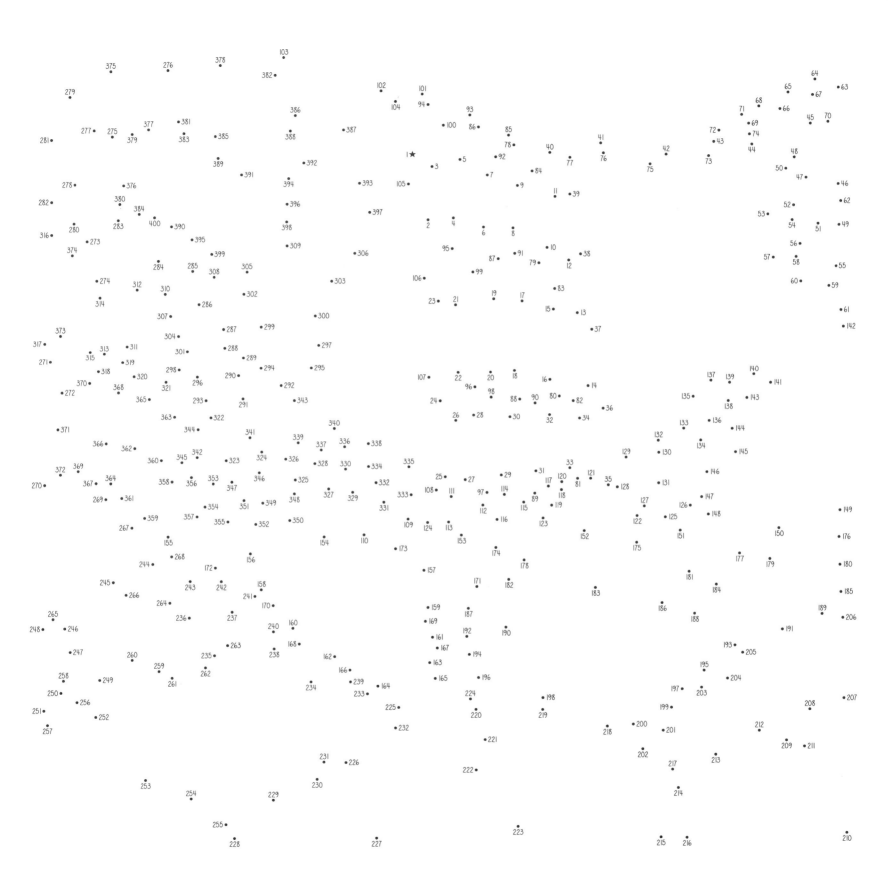

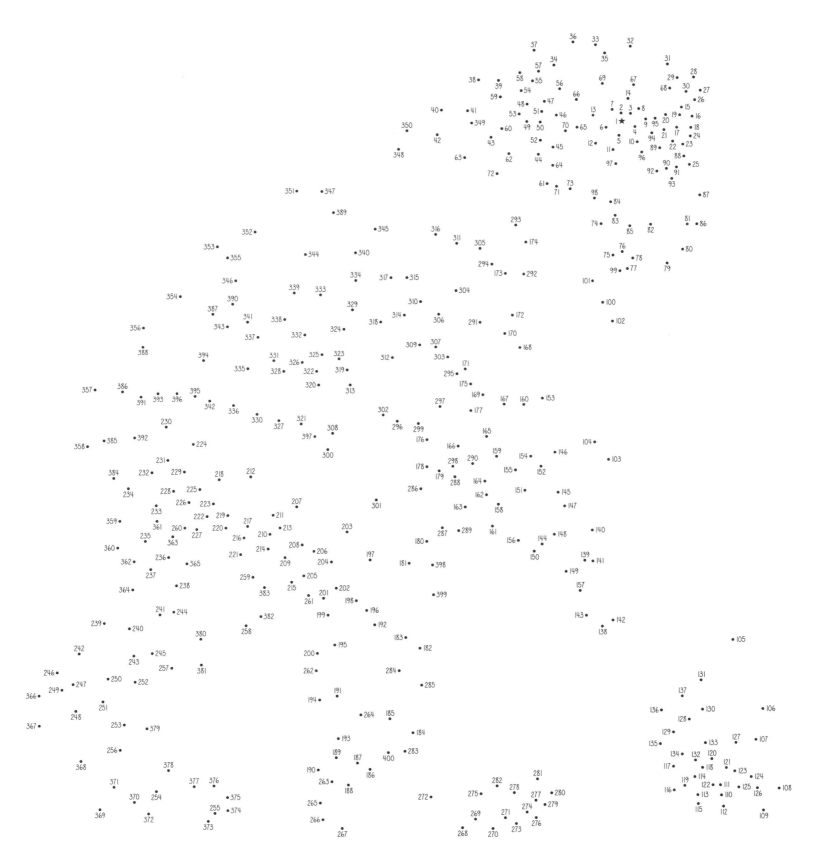

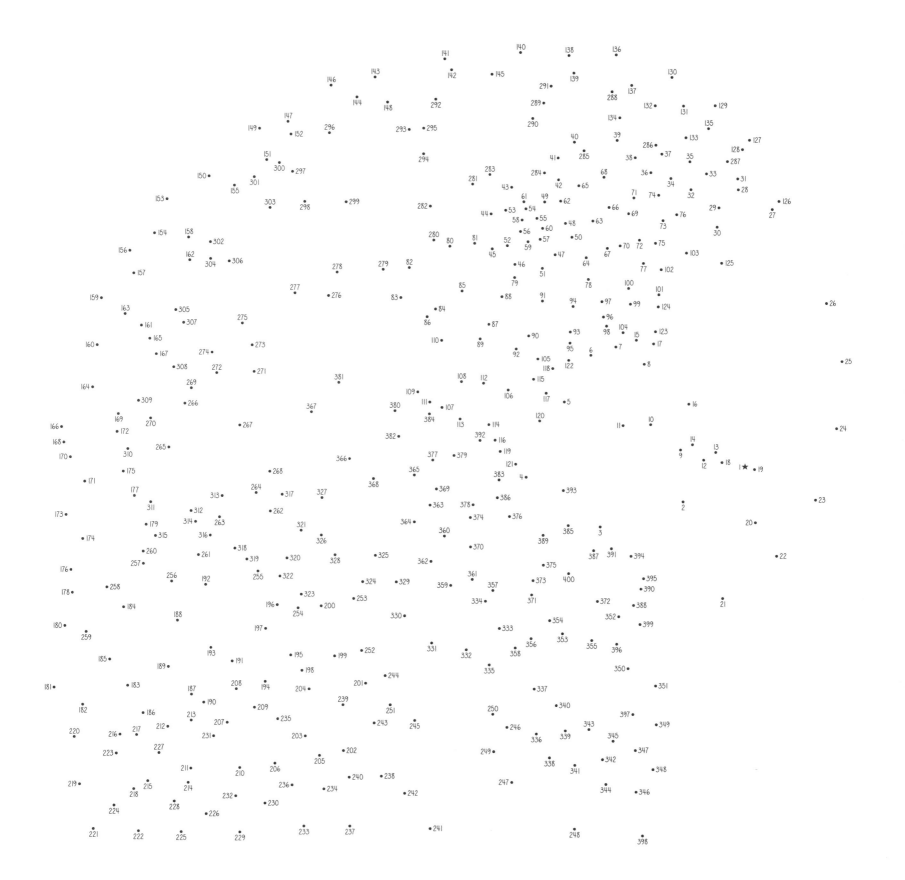

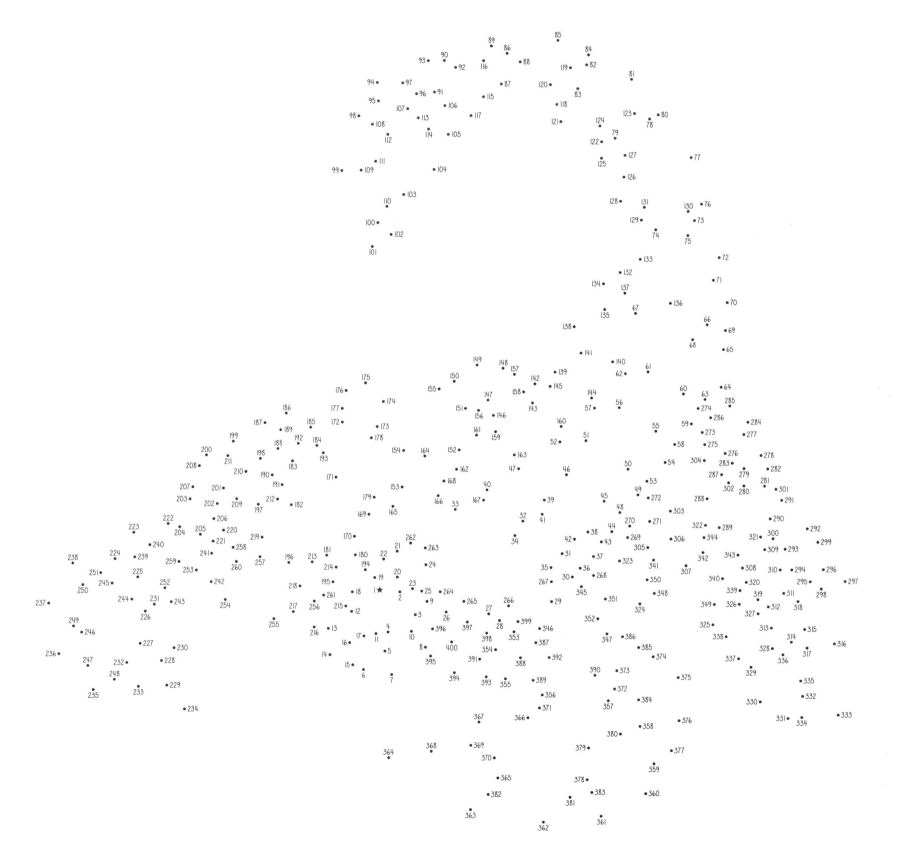

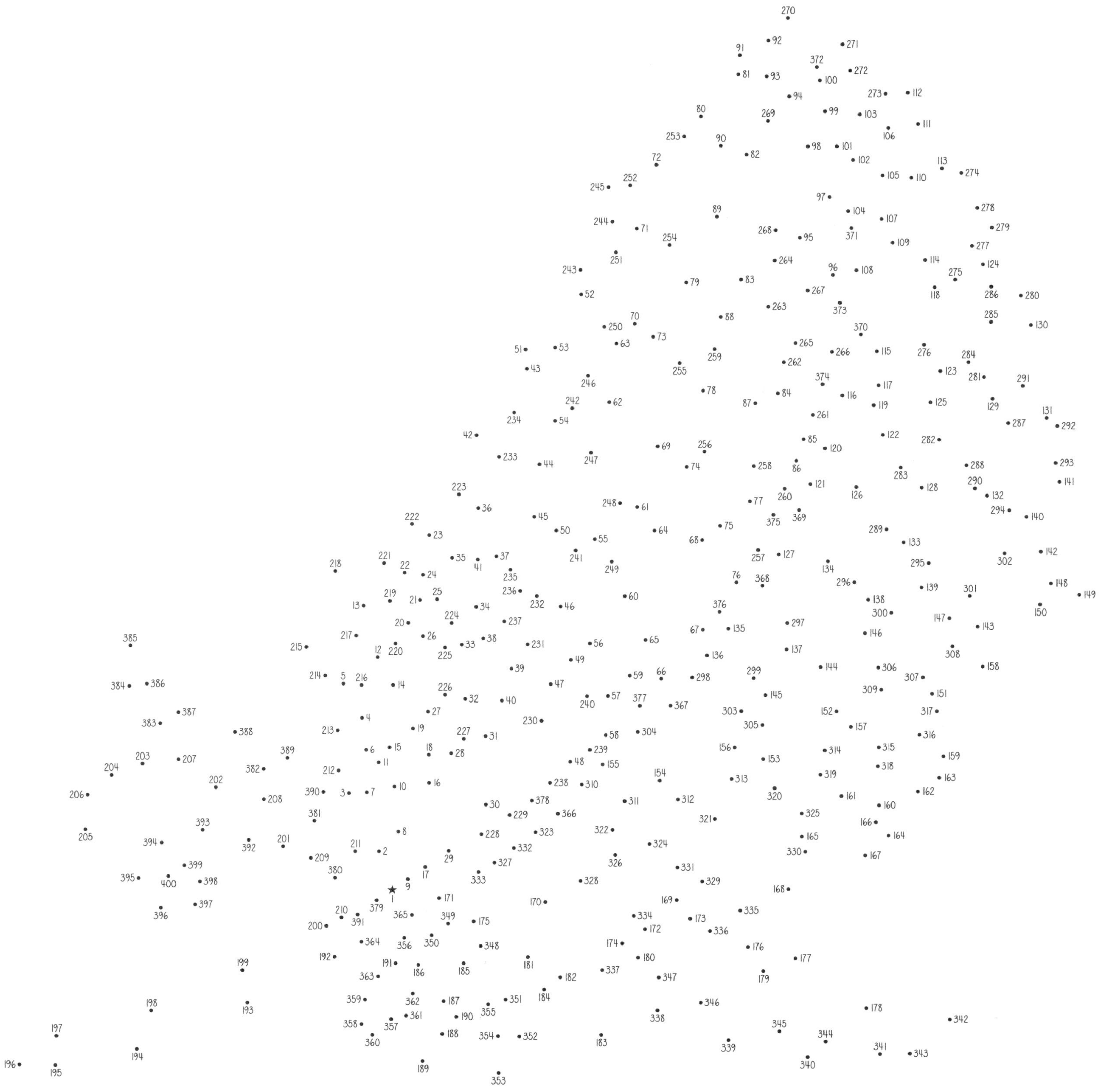

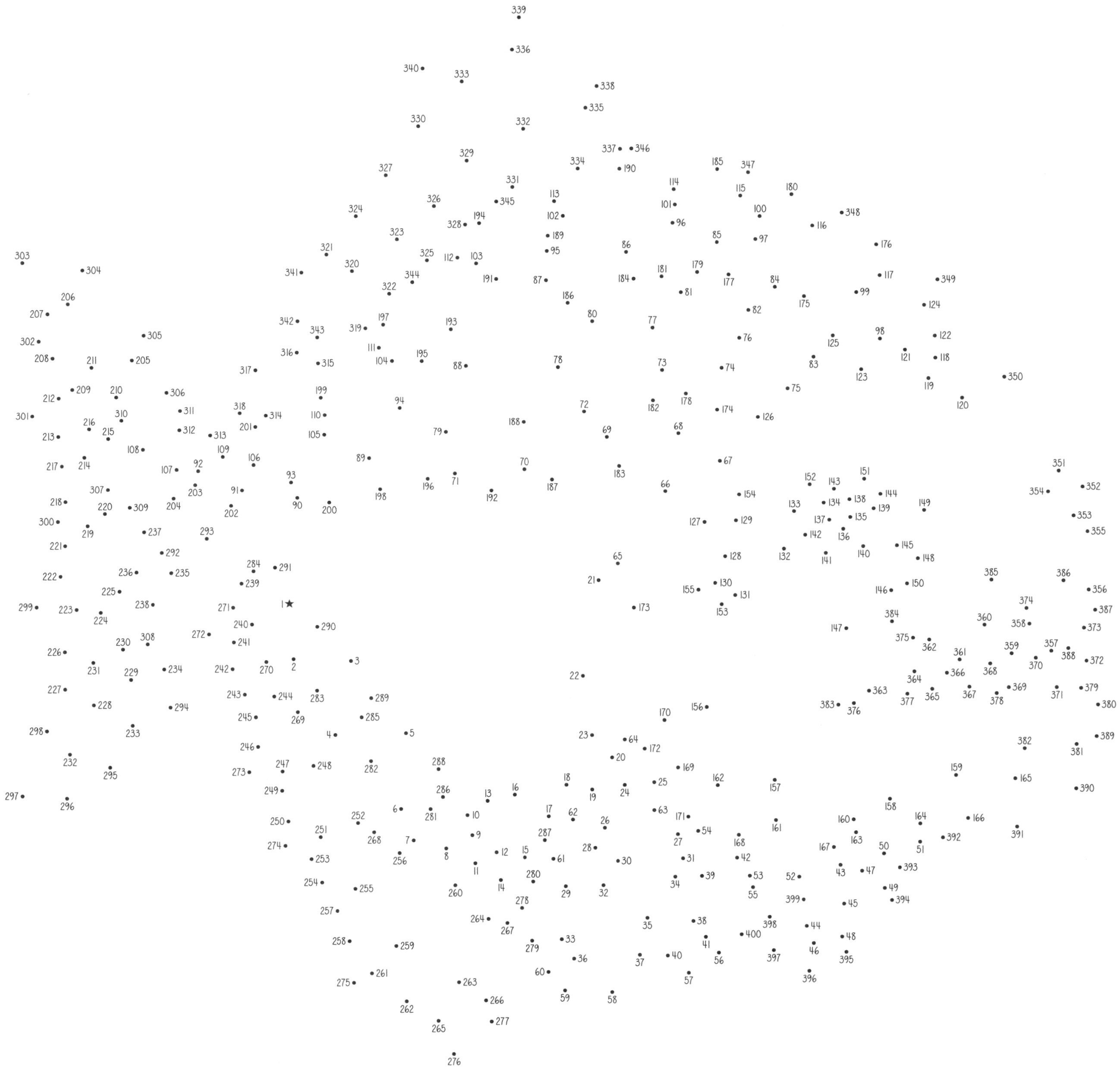

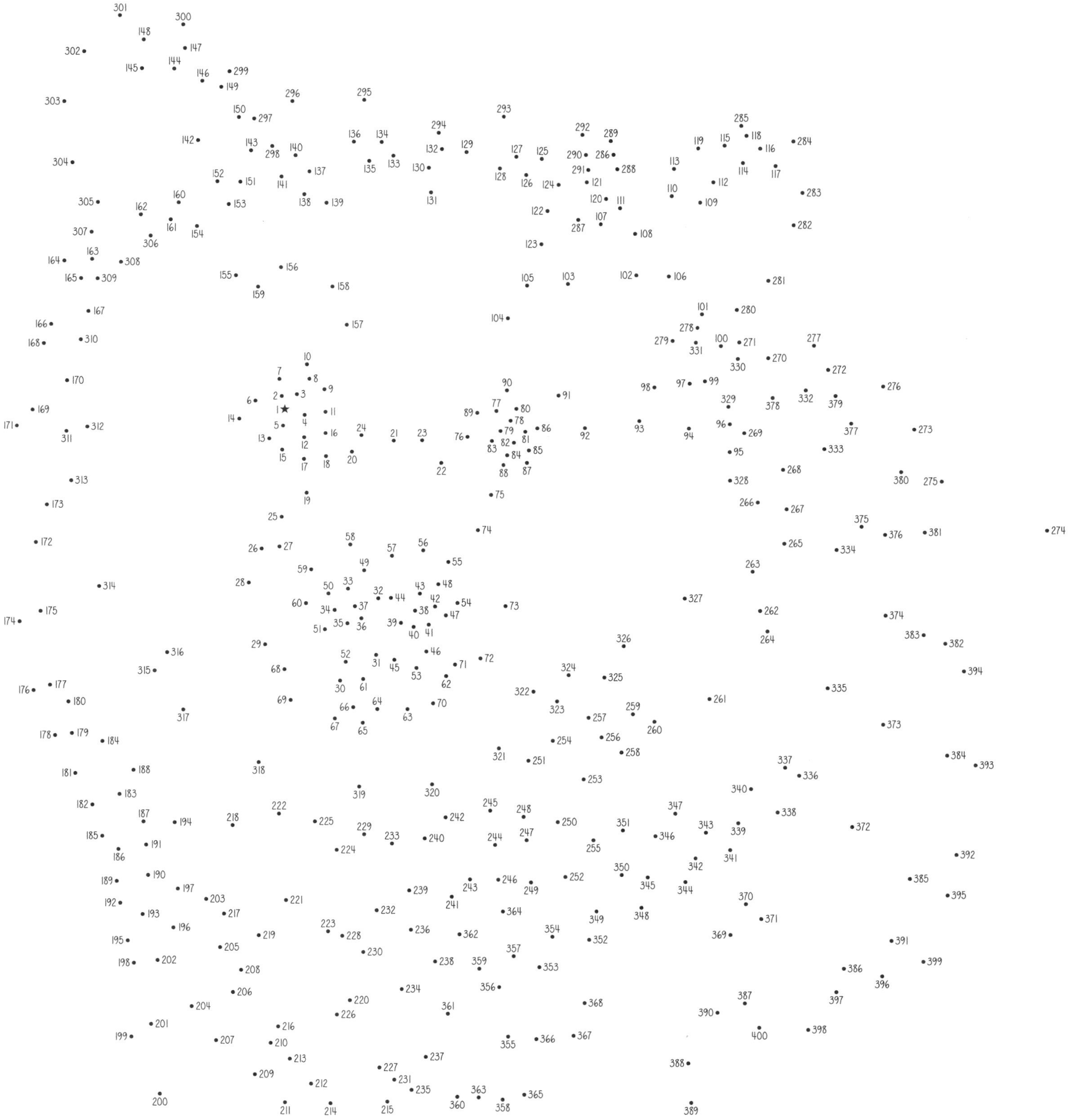

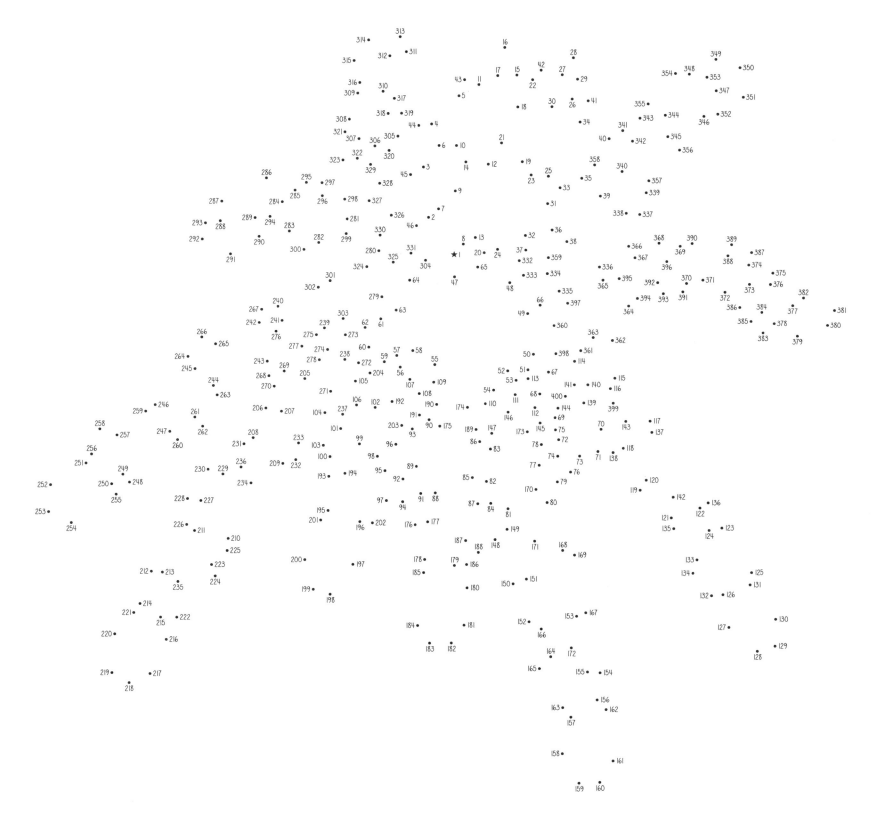

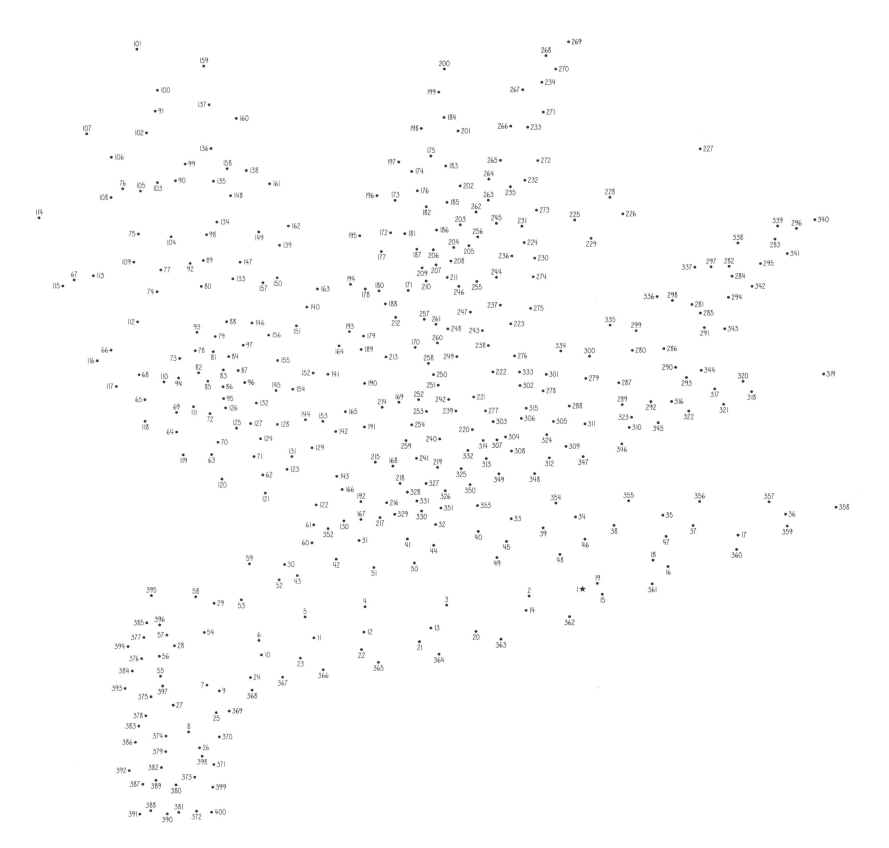

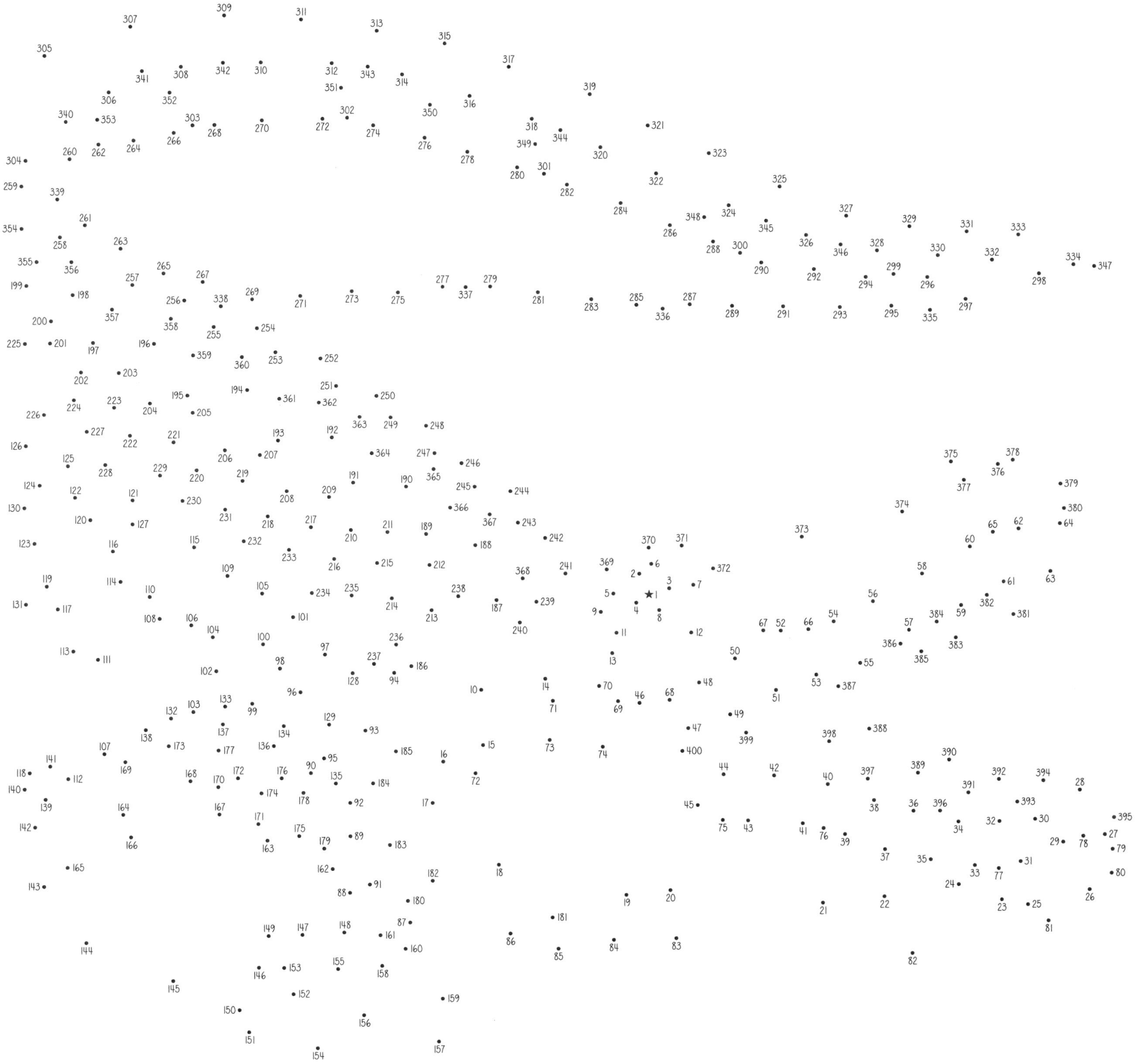

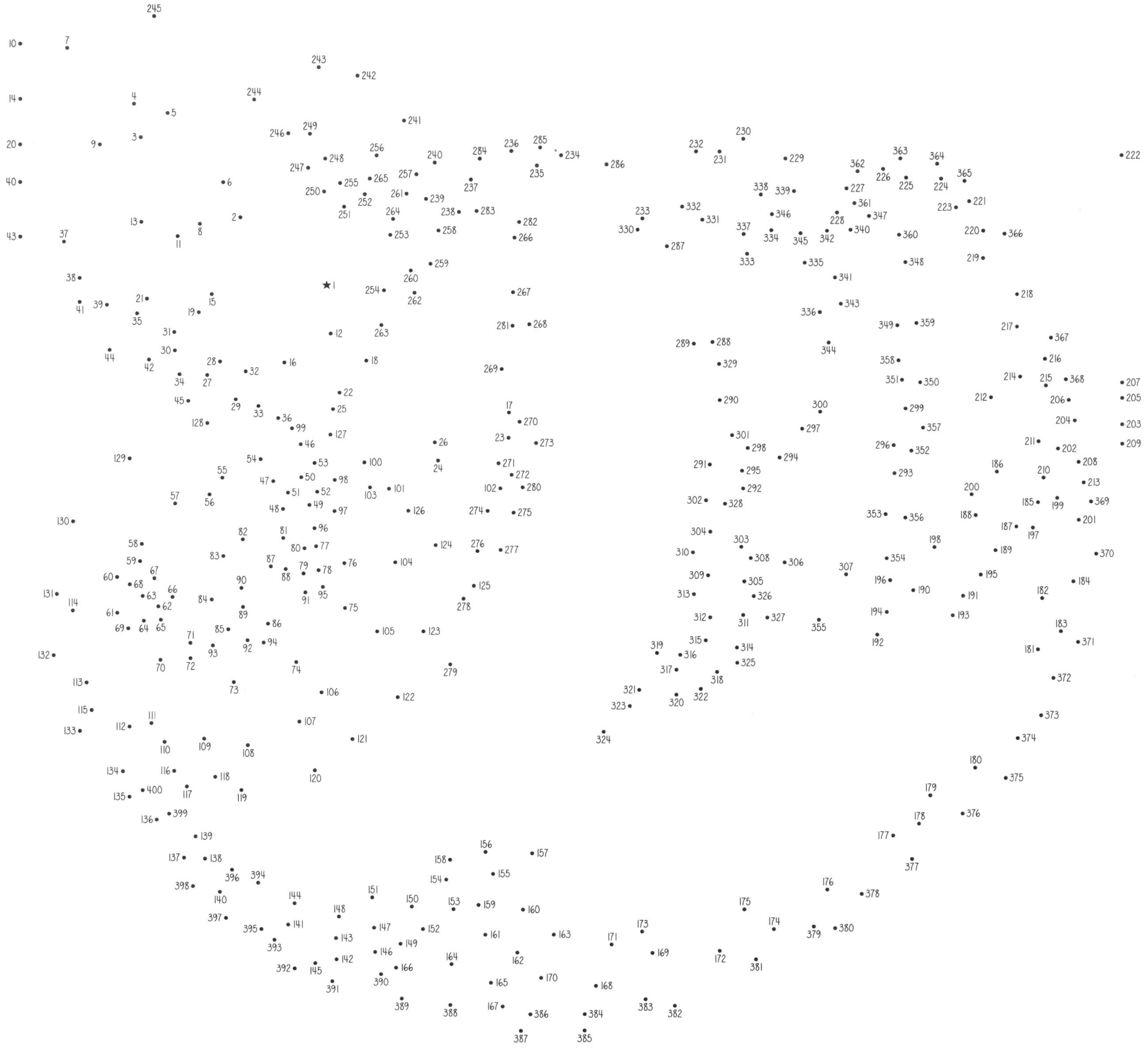

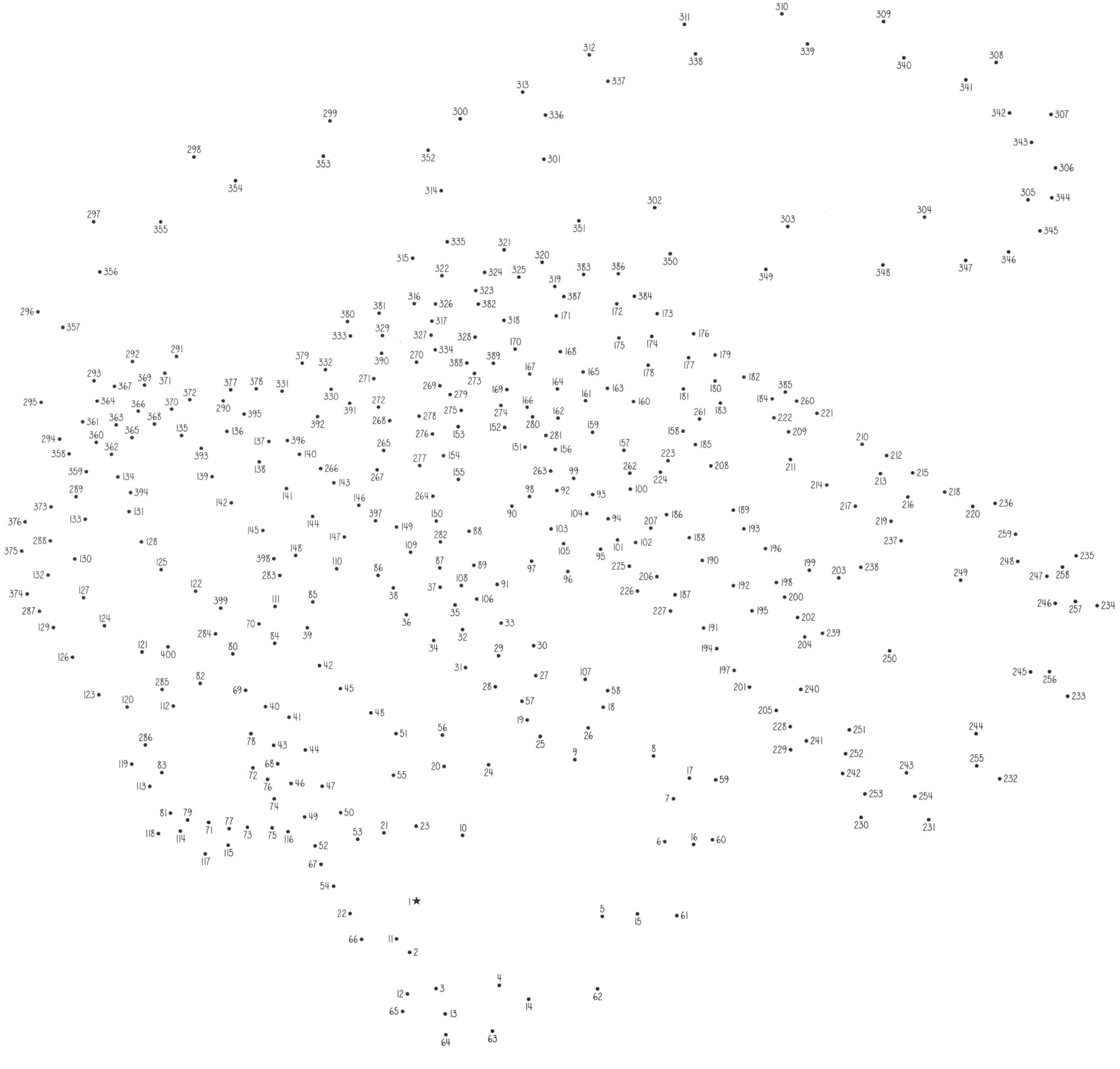

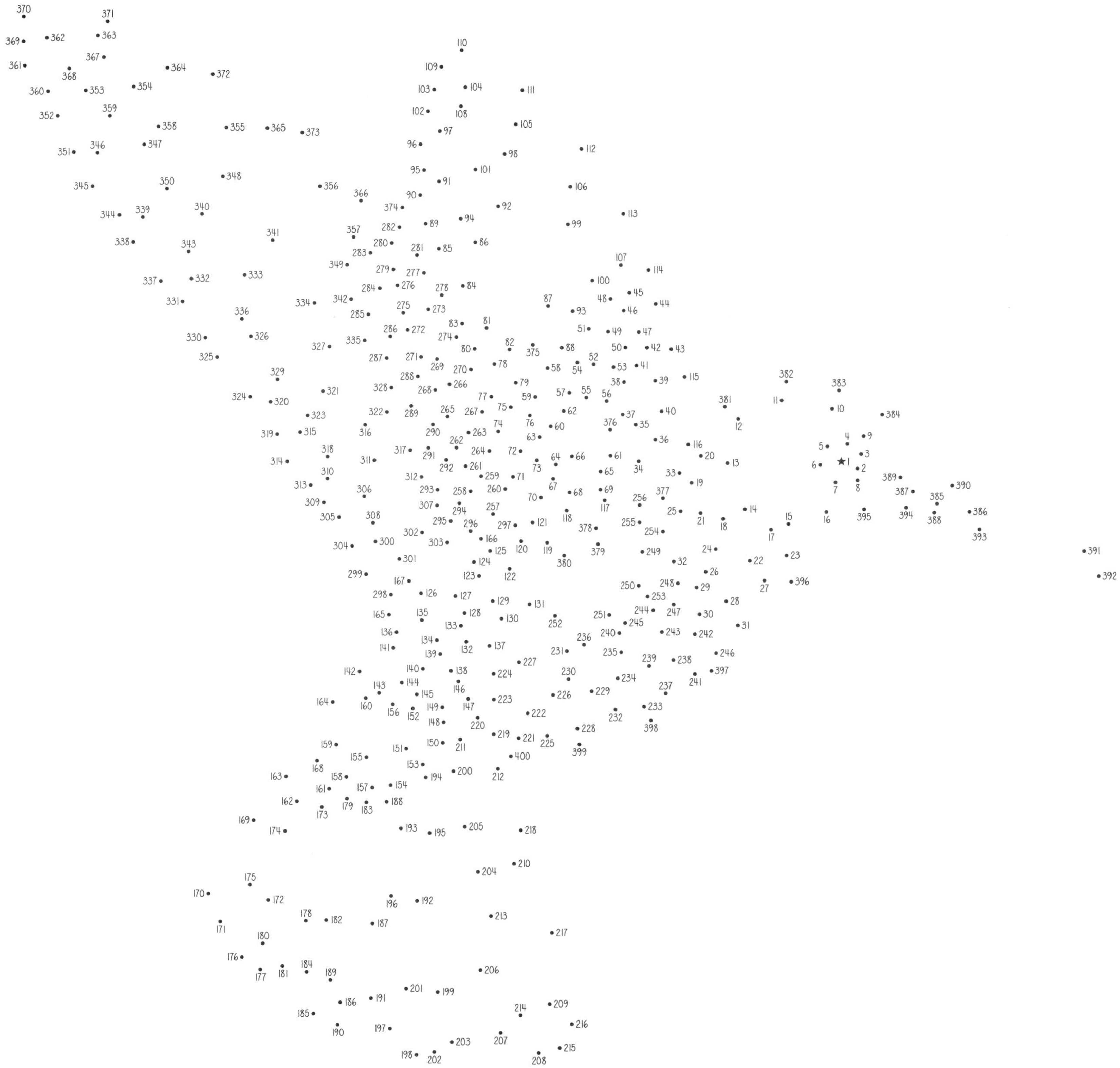

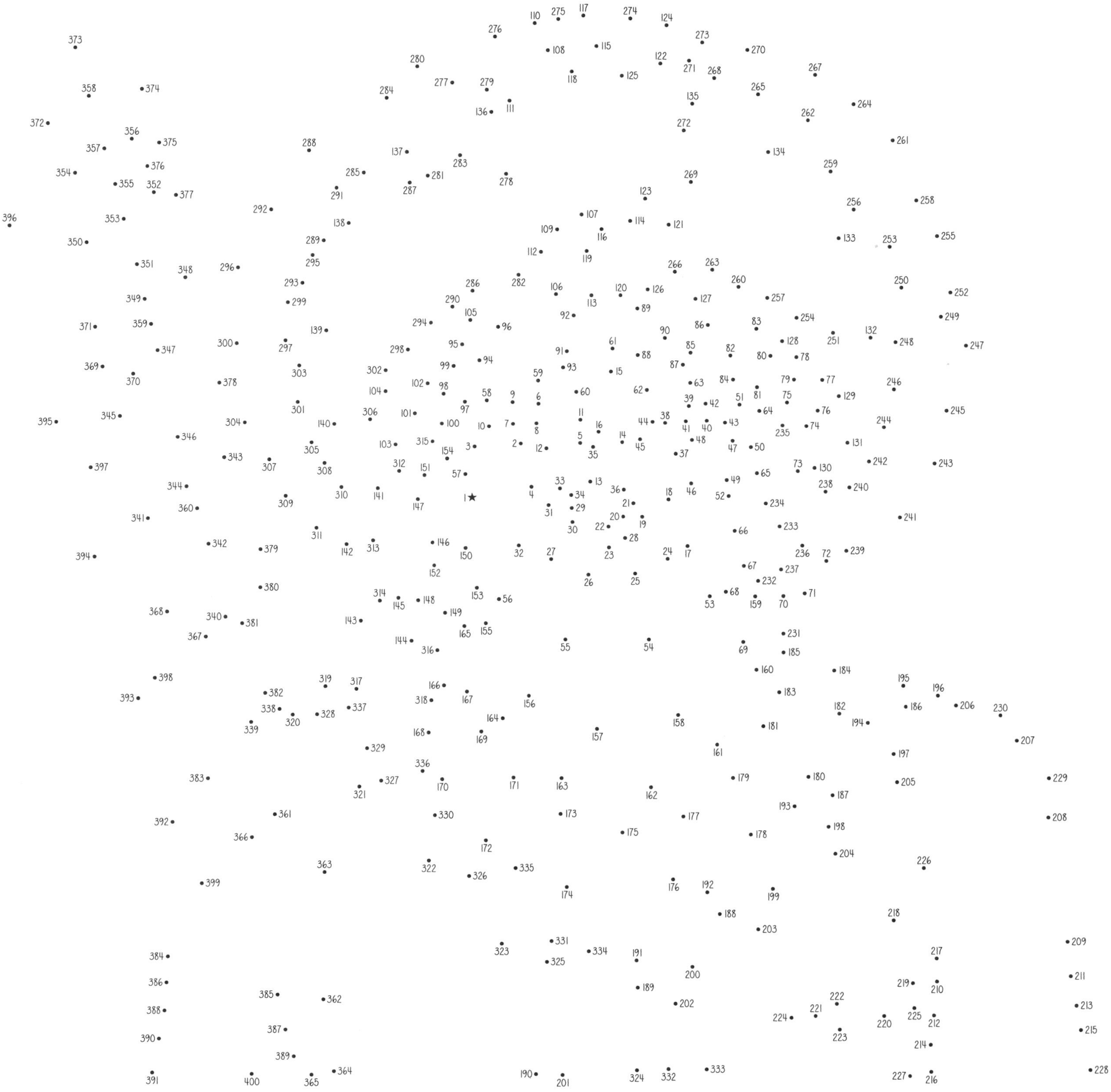

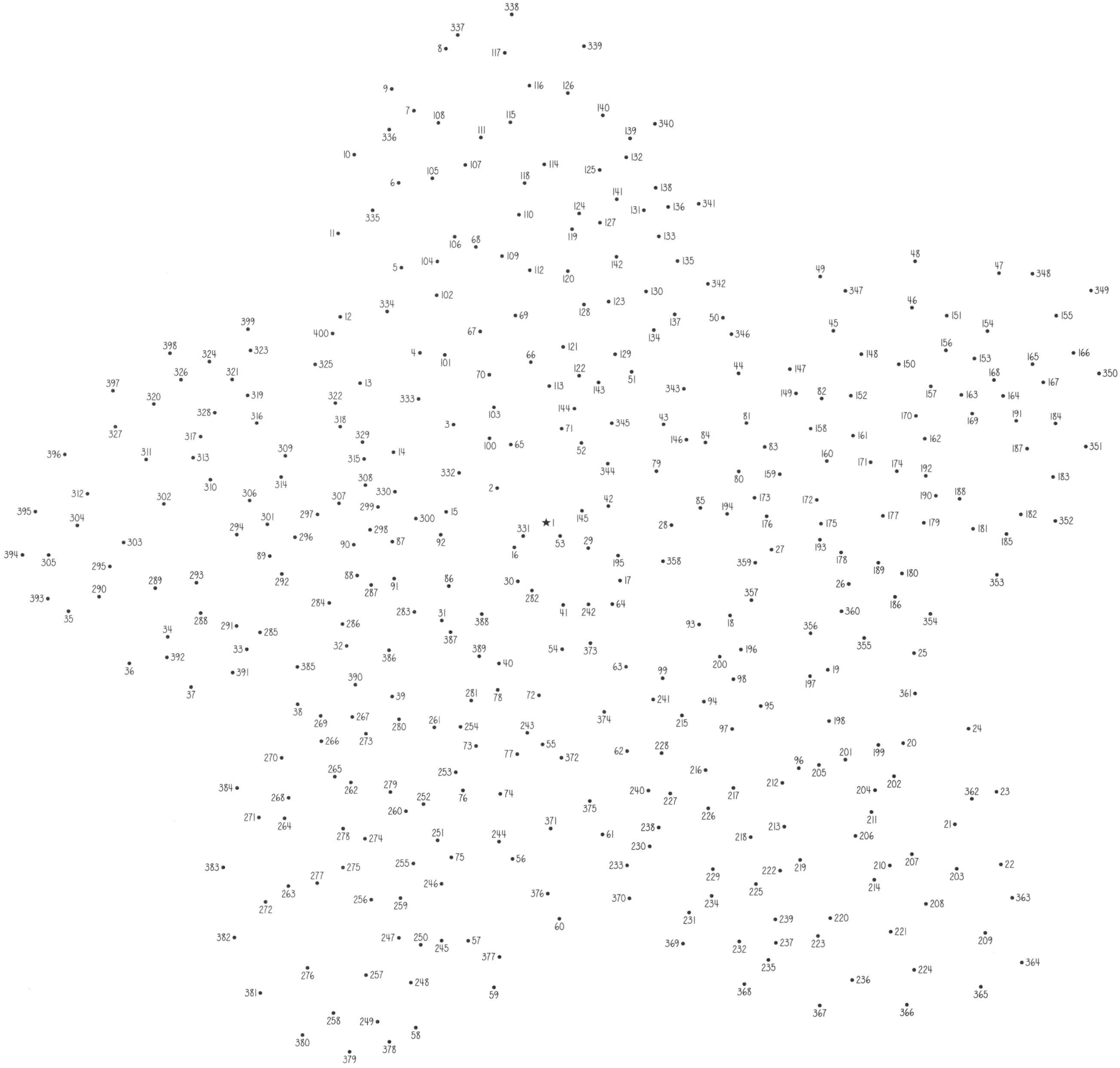

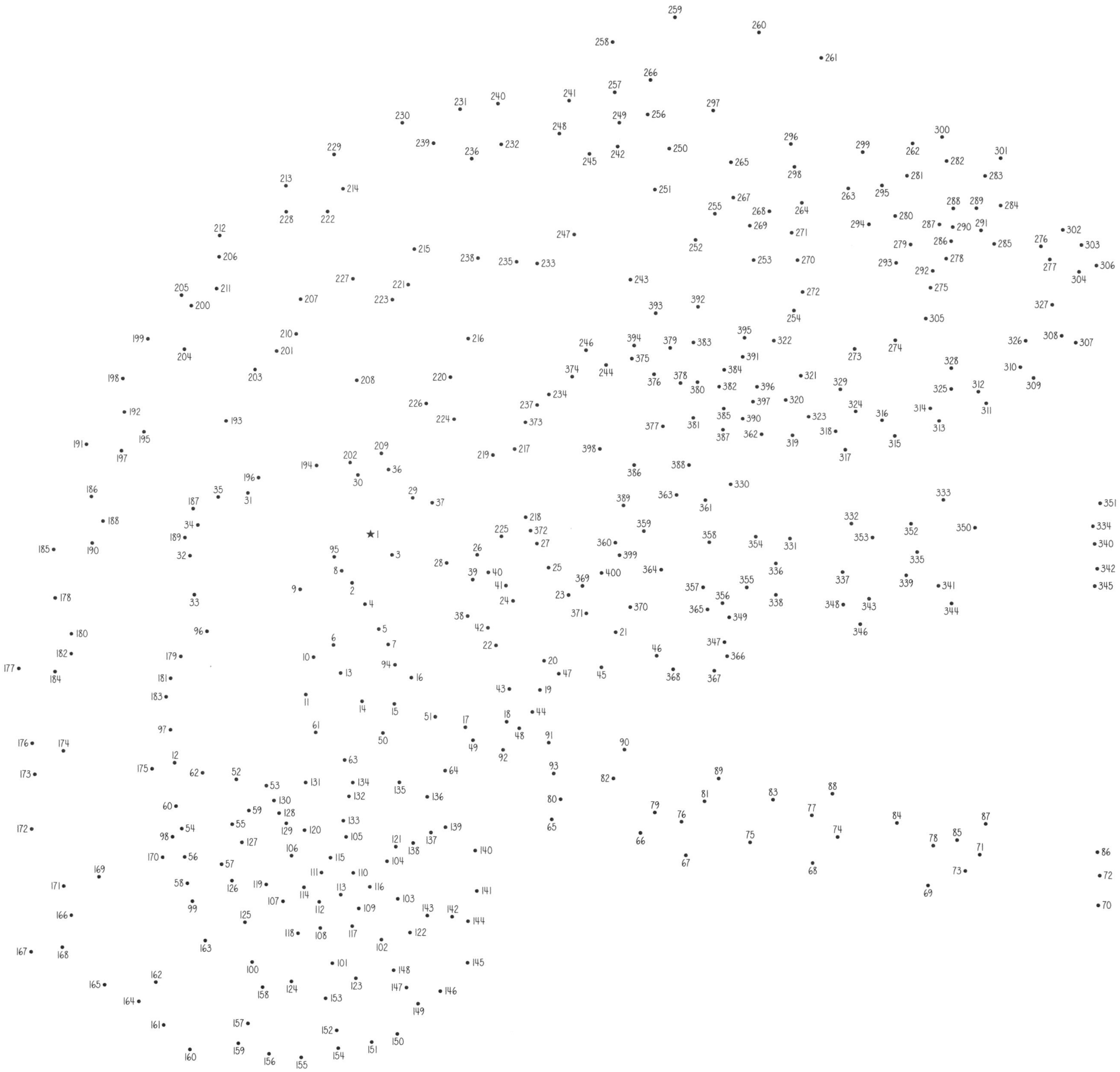

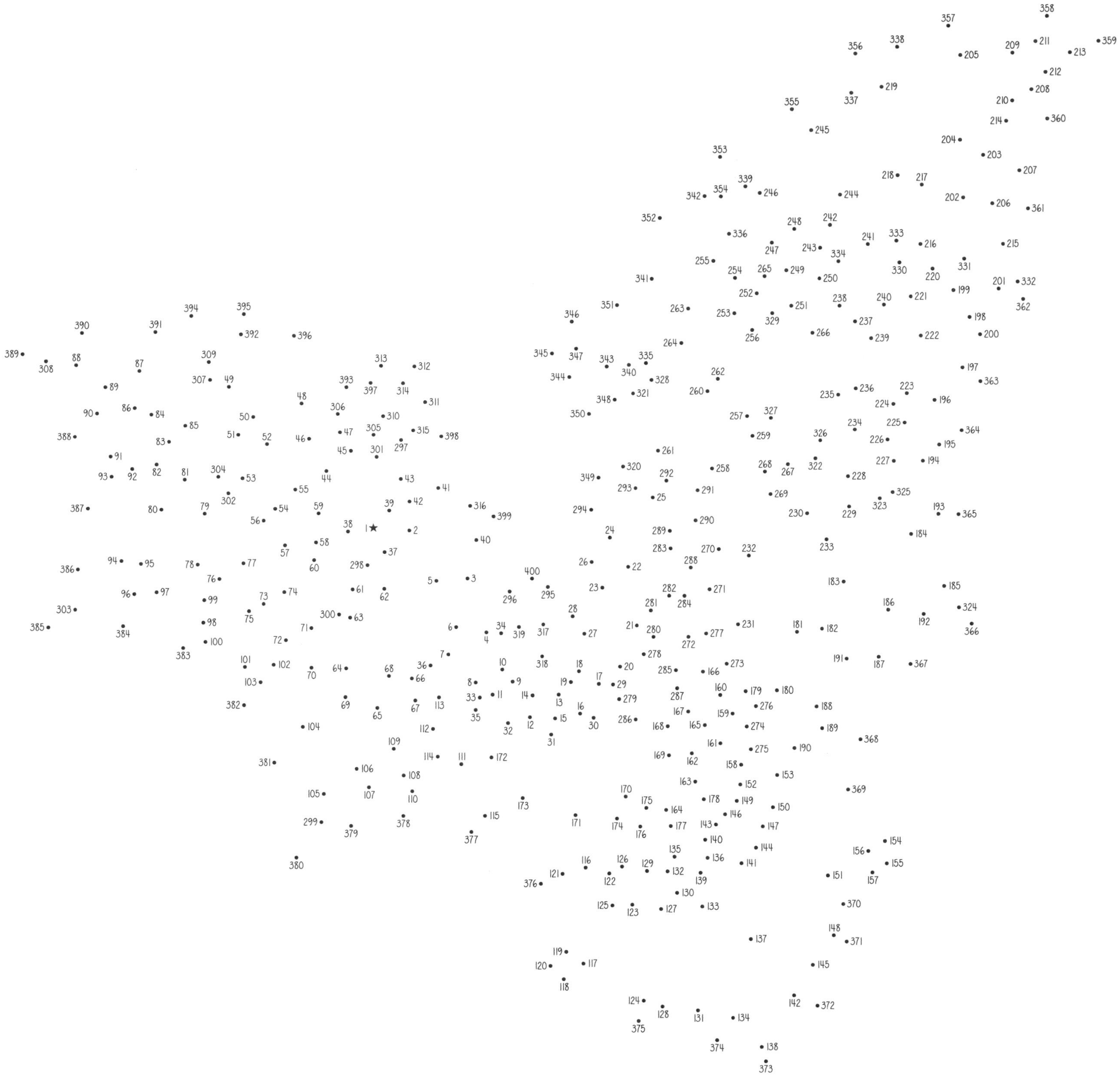

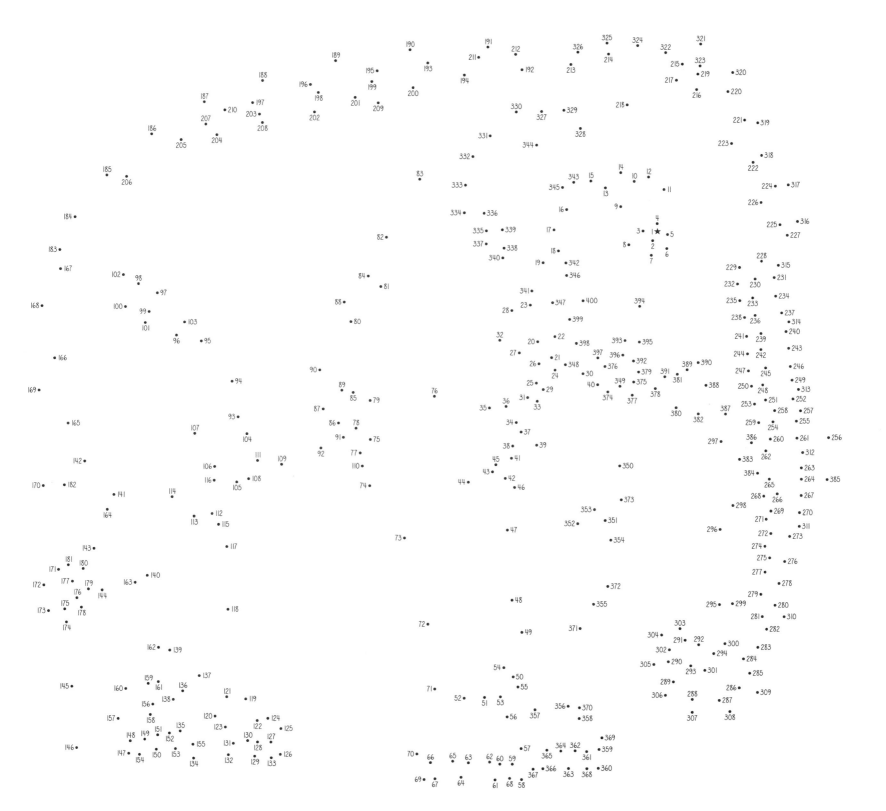

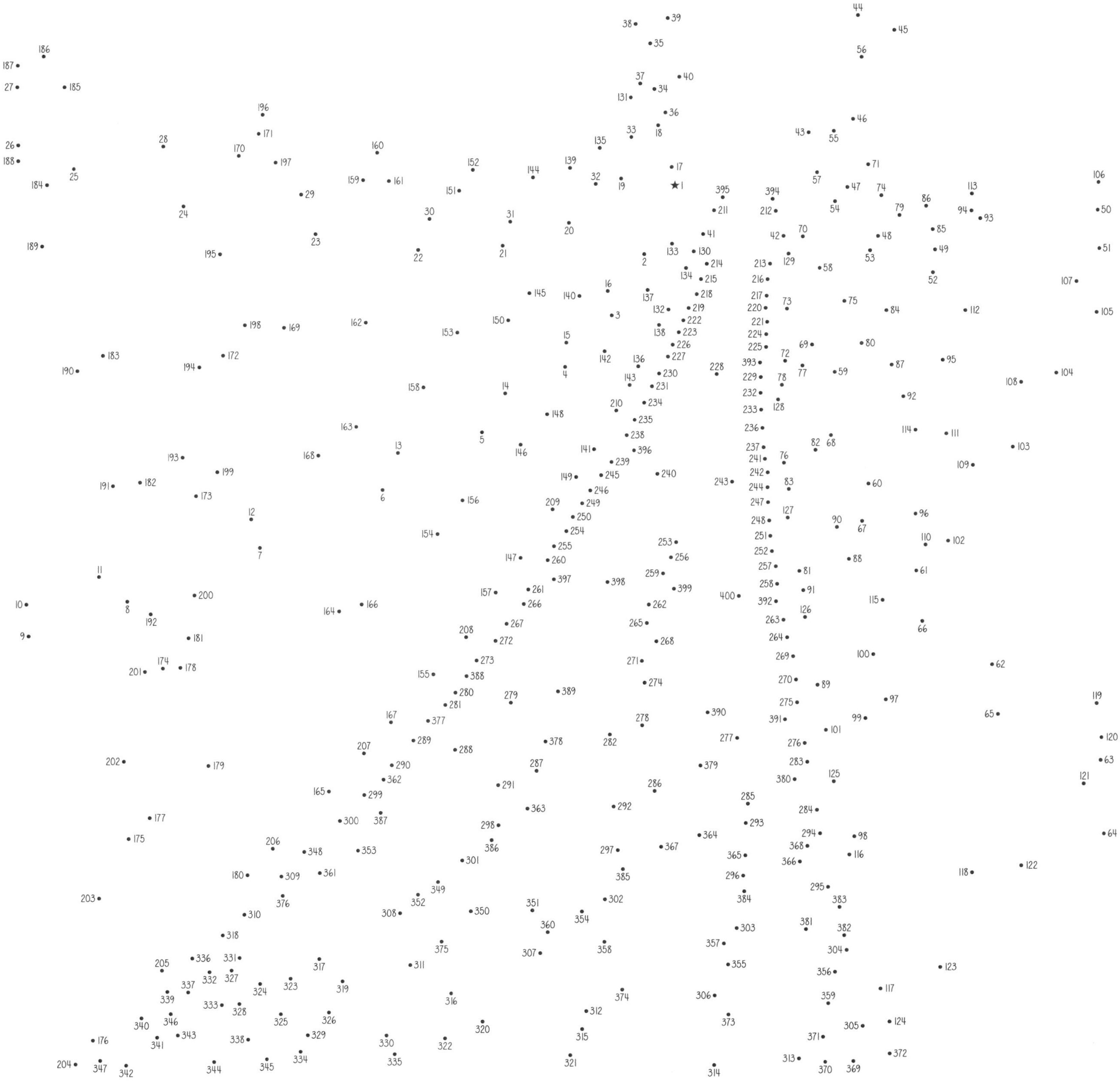

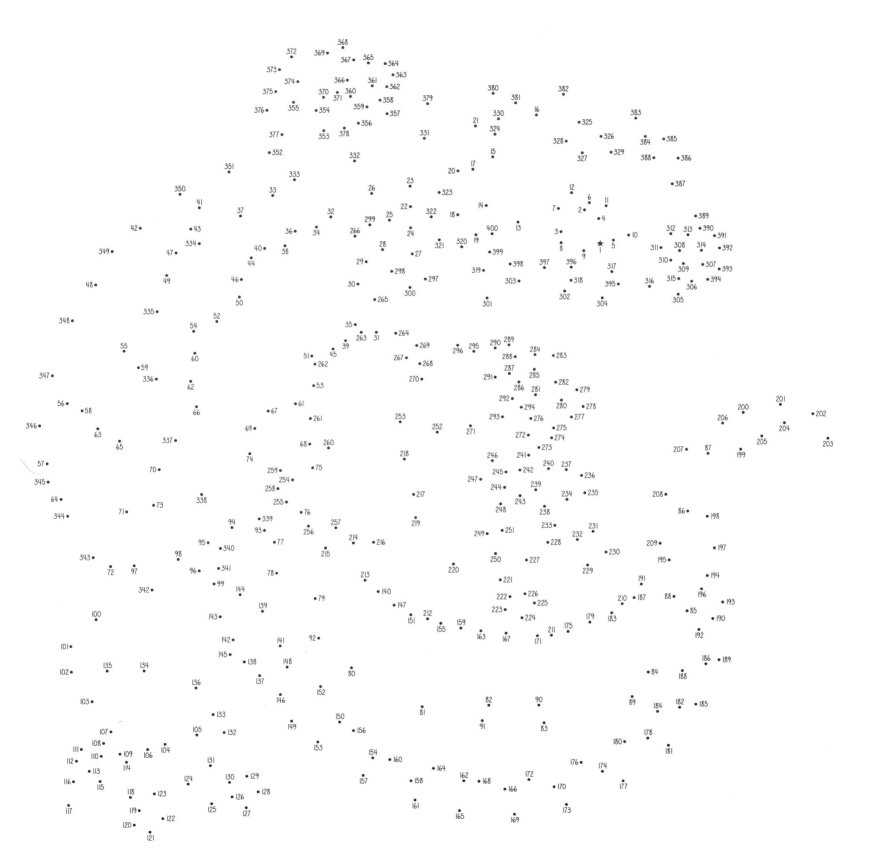

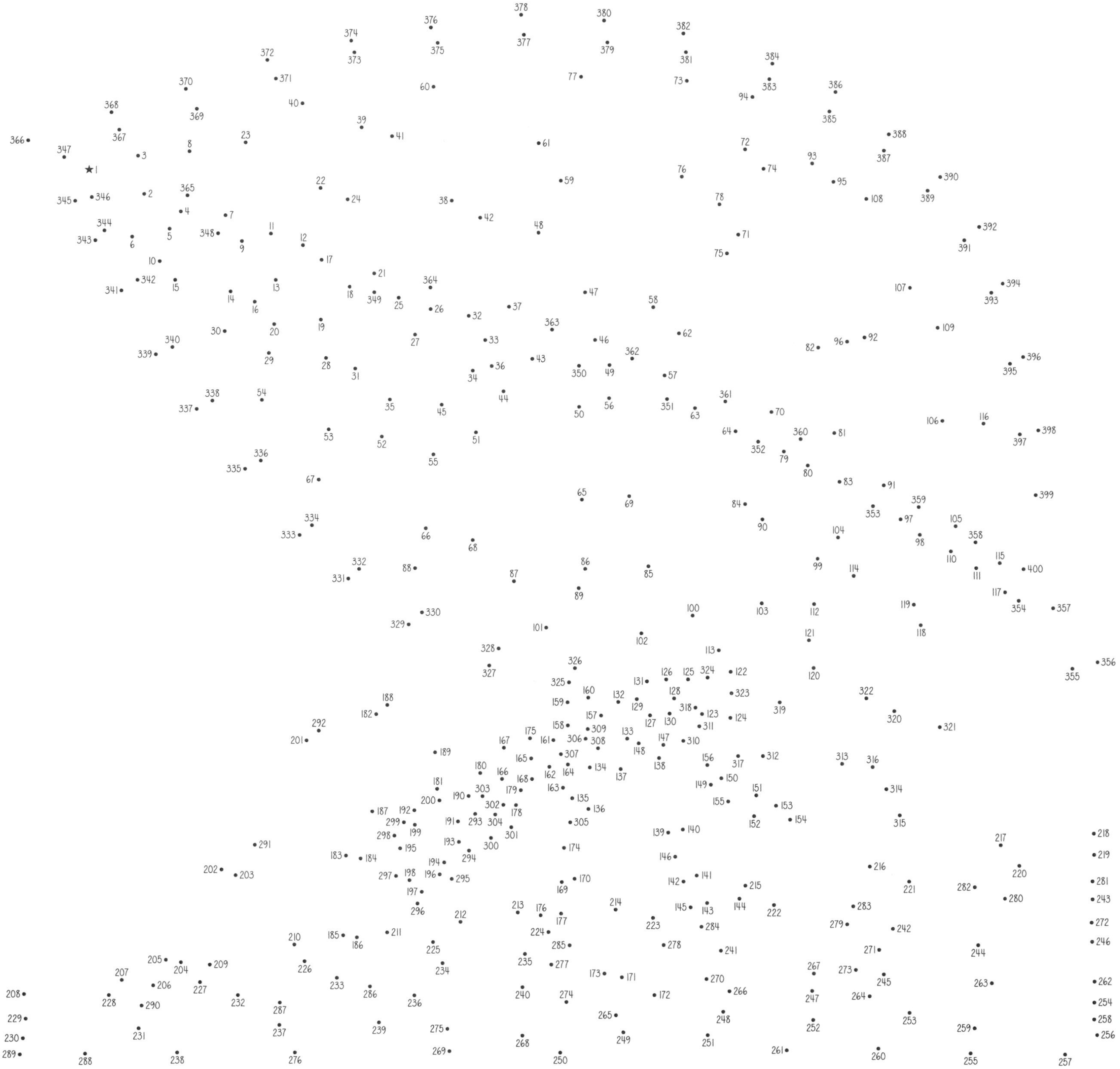

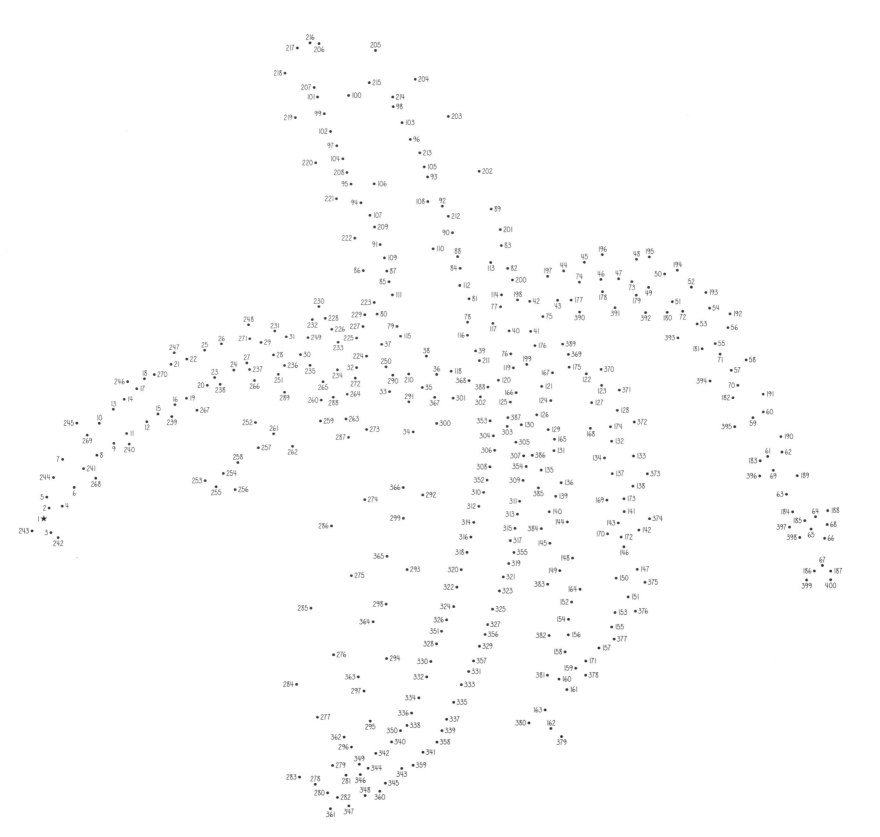

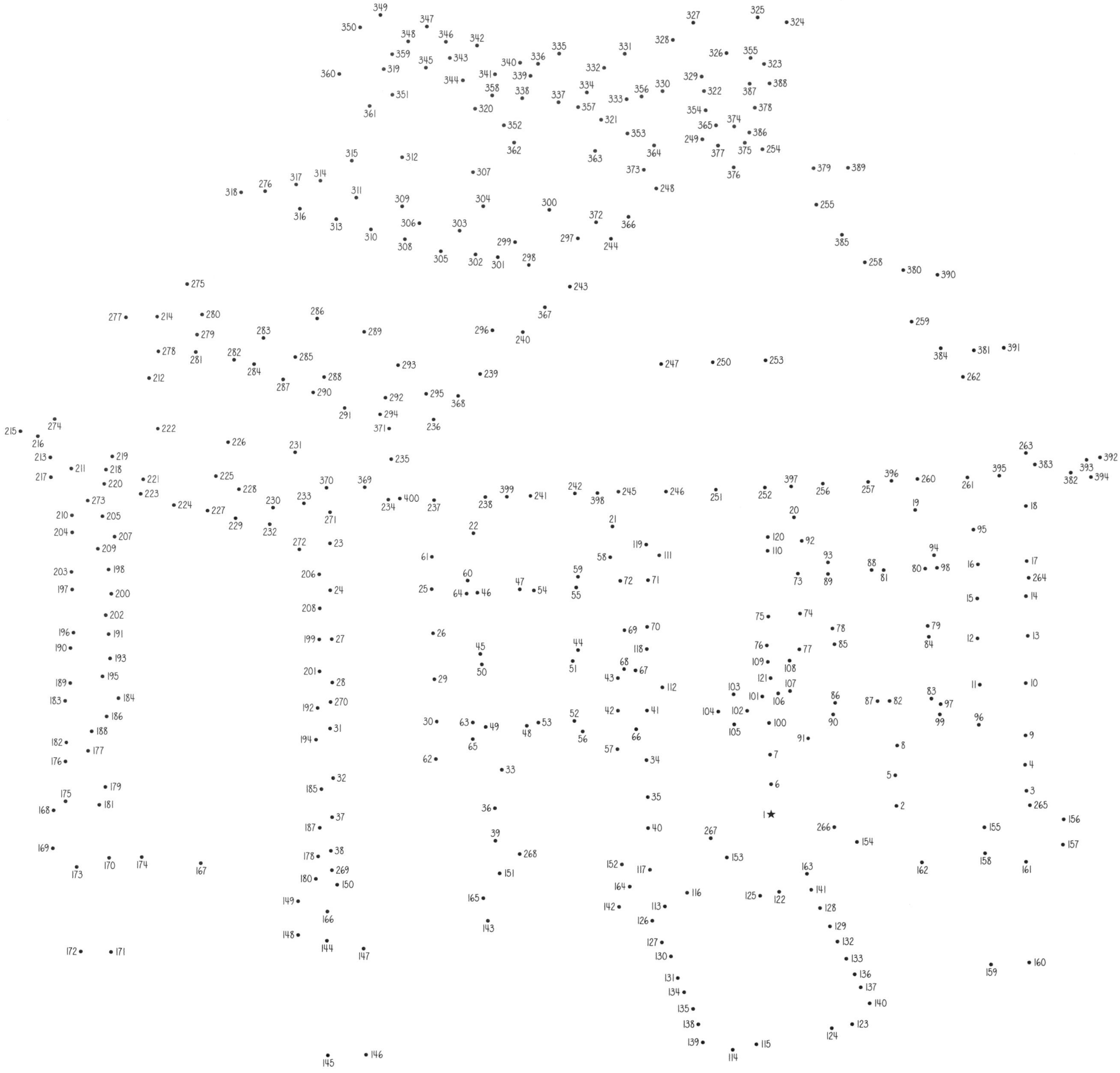

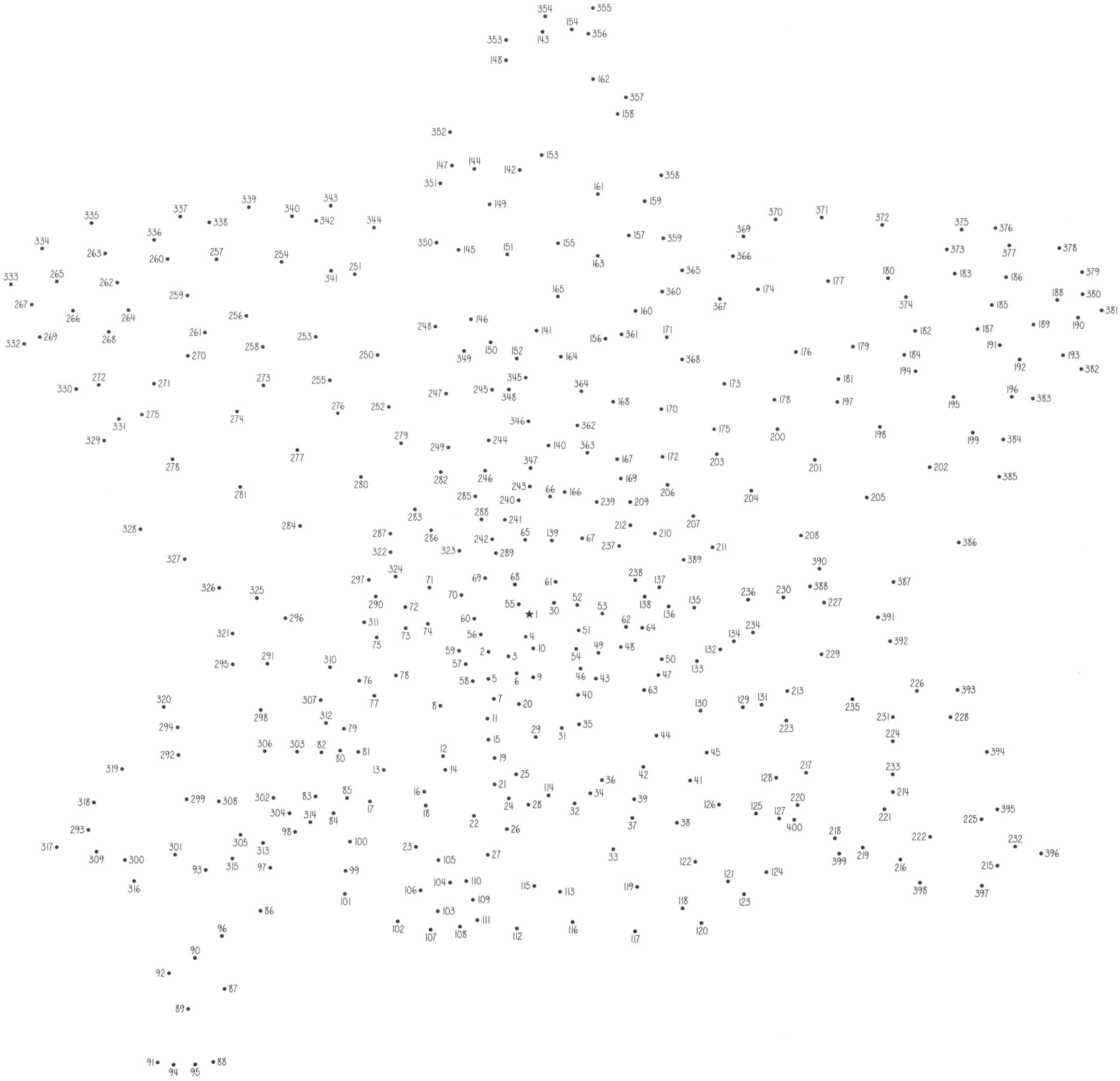

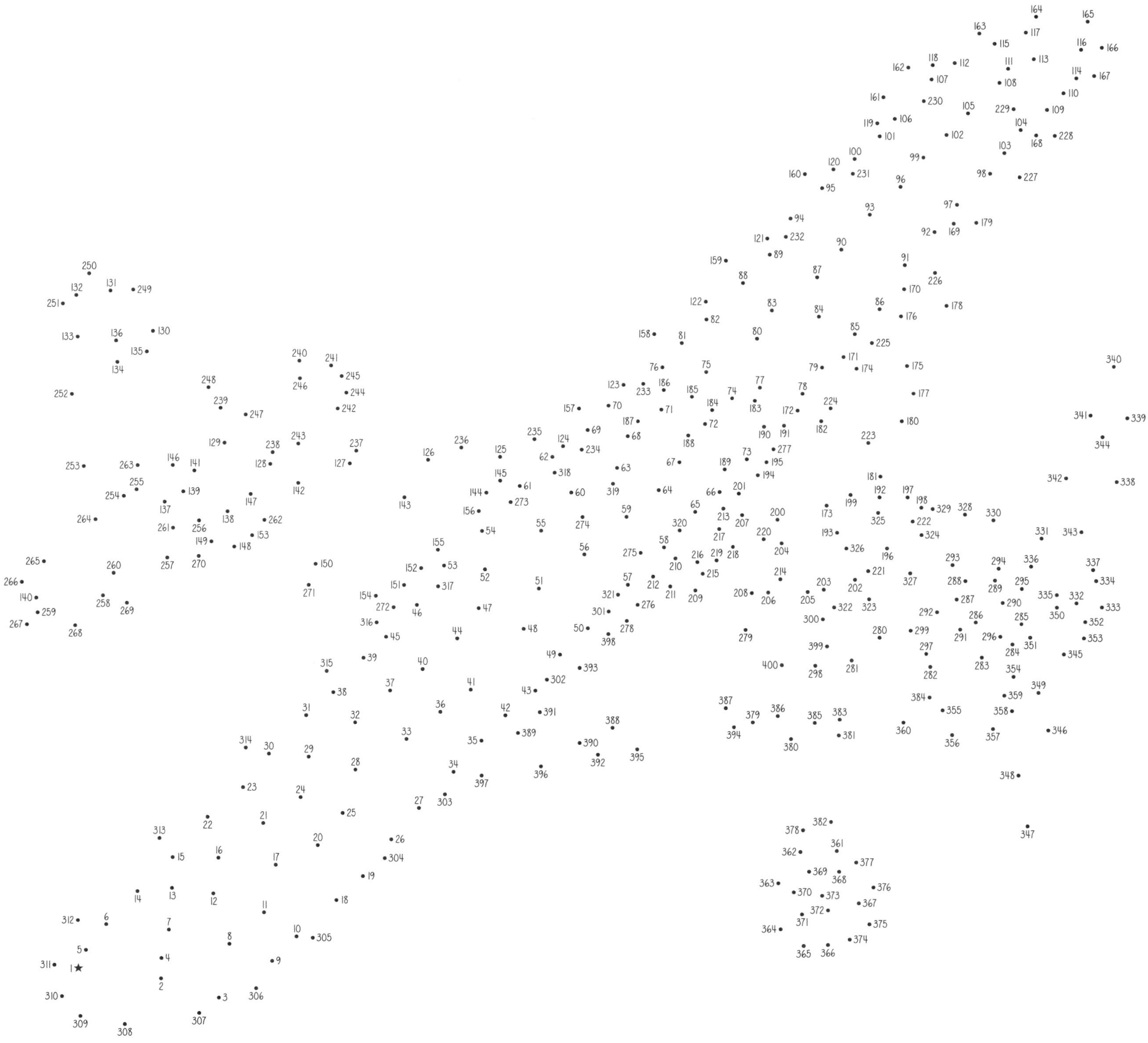

List of images

1. Butterfly
2. Toucan
3. Tiger
4. Monstera Leaf
5. Tree Frog
6. Snake
7. Water Lily
8. Snail
9. Off Road Vehicle
10. Harpy Eagle
11. Spider web
12. Fern
13. Beetle
14. Waterfall
15. Chimpanzee
16. Parrot
17. Scorpion
18. Leopard
19. Feather
20. Piranha

21. Black Bear

22. Explorer

23. Tarantula

24. Bird of Paradise Flower

25. Crocodile

26. Sloth

27. Binoculars

28. Hummingbird

29. Tribesman

30. Plumeria Flower

31. Chameleon

32. Bat

33. Elephant

34. Rope Bridge

35. Gecko

36. Ant

37. Banana

38. Monkey

39. Dragonfly

40. Canoe

41. Wooden Hut

42. Orchid

43. Aeroplane

Thanks

A special thank you to my wonderful husband Lewis
for your constant help and support.